MY BOO

"Ome...
legendary. If anyone had a question it was always Omer who provided the answer, not from a book, but from his memory. He would fascinate the people with stories of his experiences involving Nascar throughout the years." - Marie Fischer, NY

"Omer can tell stories that I could only dream about. If you ever get to meet Omer the first thing you will hear is YEEHAWEE!" - Jim Johnson, IN

"There are writers that write about the topic at hand and then there's writers who actually live(s)(d) the topic at hand. There's a whole different feeling in your articles compared to a writer who hasn't lived the words written." - Dan DEI fan, NY

"I've never come across another book - and believe me, I've read lots of them! - that gets into the personal side of the drivers, crews, owners, and fans of the greatest spectator sport anywhere." - Karen Walker, AZ

"You say you're not a career author but, your web page, book previews and approach is the best I have have ever seen. You are a TOP NOTCH author in my mind." - Rickey Champion, KY

"With forty six years attending races he can take you from the days of Fireball Roberts and David Pearson into the appearance of a brash young rookie named Dale Earnhardt, Ralph's son." - Dave R. Porter, NC

"Omer never really cared if it was a Dodge, Chevy, or Ford in front as long as he was watching what he loved to watch the most. Thank You Omer Champion, for being that "champion" that I know." - Jeffery Dye, KY

"Omer not only answers your question, but he can give all of the details that I would stay up all night to hear while sitting around his campfire" - Roger Malding, FL

"I thought I knew Nascar, but after meeting Omer, I found out that I was a rookie" - Craig Newsome, GA

"Just thinking about the Fireball, Fastback Freddy, LeeRoy,Little Bud Moore, 'Lil Joe, Rex White, Curtis & Co.brings a smile to my face" - JanGames, OH

CREDITS, COPYRIGHT AND DISCLAIMERS

"NASCAR YeeHawee Style"
Omer Champion, Author

ISBN 0-9755050-0-9

Published by Omer Champion
P. O. Box 128
Thornton, KY. 41855

Printed by Color House Graphics
3505 Eastern Ave. S.E.
Grand Rapids, MI 49508

Cover and interior design by Bryan Auxier

Cover photo by Mickey Weinstein,
www.instantreplaysportscard.com

Photo Credits are shown in the caption section of the picture.

A Special Thanks to my family and friends who supported me during the writing of this book.

I Proudly dedicate this book to my brother, Rickey Champion.

Dedicated with pride. It gives me great pride and pleasure to dedicate this book to my brother Rickey Champion. I will never forget the first time that Rickey and I went to a race together. Rickey was only 6 years old when we went to the Firecracker 250 at Daytona. What a thrill it was to look into his big excited eyes as Fireball Roberts went streaking by for the first time. On that day Rickey was totally hooked on Nascar racing. It is impossible for me to tell you how many races (about 200) we attended together, but I can truly say the happiest racing days of my life were spent with him. I am 15 years older than Rickey and I sometimes feel like his daddy. BTW, did you notice that Rickey was kneeling down in the picture? I bet he is getting ready to beg me to take him to another race. Rickey, here is a big special YeeHawee for you and always remember that I love you.

Photo by Becky Champion

FOREWORD

"NASCAR YeeHawee Style" was written By Omer Champion, a Kentucky Hillbilly with more than 46 years of NASCAR racing experience. If you think you "HAVE GOT IT BAD" now, just wait until you read "NASCAR YeeHawee Style".

The book is very professionally written, but has a slight touch of Redneck Happiness. Written in a very unorthodox way; as only a Kentucky Hillbilly could have the courage to let you have a blast while reading it.

The book is jammed packed with personal stories experienced by Omer Champion who has attended more than 400 Nascar races. You will have to take a very deep breath as the excitement and fun overwhelms you and causes you to want more.

The book has a very broad format and covers almost everything that a fan has seen, experienced or wanted to know about. Here are some of the topics that you will enjoy: It is about stories, campgrounds, parties, infields, hall of fames, beads, fights, wrecks, hot tempers, big red trailer, wild times, loving family, personal aspects of drivers and their families, trivia, did you know, poems, dangerous happenings, my opinions, my yeehawee friends opinions, Nascar games, potluck fun and a Dale Earnhardt Tribute. For the very first time, I am introducing a chapter called Dale Earnhardt Pro and Con which gives the friends and foe alike a chance to voice their opinion of the MAN. You are going to love this book and when you finish reading it, you will look up with a big happy smile on your face and yell YEEEHAWEE.

Thank you. Omer Champion

TABLE OF CONTENTS

The Author   8

My Stories   21

Potluck   82

Trivia   108

Dale Earnhardt Pro and Con   121

Games   141

My Friends Stories   152

Poems   202

My Opinions   210

Did You Know?   221

Pictures   242

INTRODUCING THE AUTHOR

Written by: Marie Fischer

You'd be fortunate if once or twice, during your lifetime, you met a person that you felt an instant rapport with. That person for me is the author of this book, Omer Champion. I met him on the Internet a few years back on a NG (Newsgroup) list where the participants were Nascar racing fans. My recollection of Omer is that he was the first person to greet and welcome me into the group. I quickly learned that he was kind of the unofficial leader of the group, even though not the owner of the list. He was the one who responded to virtually every posting generated.

Only through his sense of friendship, honesty and extending a helpful hand had Omer become a confident to many of his extended Internet family. As a group we came to know his personal family including his beloved wife, Jo, happy that they are willing to share Omer with us. His knowledge of Nascar racing is almost legendary. If anyone had a question it was always Omer who provided the answer, not from a book, but from his memory. He would fascinate the people with stories of his experiences involving Nascar throughout the years.

Omer was born and raised in Kentucky. I guess you could call him one of the "good old boys". As a young man he attended Nascar races locally and eventually branched out to go to races at many of the past and present day tracks. From those roots is where Omer got the facts for this book. He was fortunate enough to personally meet the racing drivers and the men who worked on their machines. Stories sprinkled with names like Richard Petty, Cale Yarborough and Curtis Turner kept the group's attention and asking for more. One of my favorites is when he got his jacket signed by Richard Petty, who will always be Omer's favorite driver.

He still attends many races throughout the year, encouraging others to join in the fun. Attesting to Omer's impact on his friends, this encouragement is developing into an annual event of a growing gathering of his friends at Bristol Motor speedway in Tennessee. Starting with a few to well over 20 people and their family members meet at a campground near the track. The overwhelming reason to get together is to meet Omer Champion and to hear his YeeHaw. I was fortunate enough to meet Omer at Bristol and is one of my most treasured memories.

The people on the NG message board come to know each other over a period of time and friendships are developed. Omer, by far, is the most respected and loved person in the group. With as many friends he has on the Internet can only attest to the amount of friends he has in his personal life. I am lucky to be able to call Omer Champion as my friend.

I'll wager that reading through this book you'll get a sense of history of Nascar racing seen through the eyes of a person whose experiences he is sharing with you. I'll also wager that you'll feel that Omer is your friend too.

Marie Fischer

By David R. Porter

PureWCup~Dave R.P.

My good friend Omer Champion is the most Knowledgeable NASCAR fan that I know. He started his learning process as a young boy on top of a Kentucky mountain. His Dad took him there because it was the only place the old car radio would pick up the race being broadcast. Those were the good old days when you could walk up to a big name driver and just have a chat next to his pickup truck. Omer will tell you how he spent forty five minutes out back of a motel with Richard Petty, his long time hero.

With forty six years attending races he can take you from the days of Fireball Roberts and David Pearson into the appearance of a brash young rookie named Dale Earnhardt, Ralph's son. Omer is a good old boy from the hills of Kentucky but he also knows his NASCAR right up into the advent of todays " Young Guns". Jeff Gordon and Dale Earnhardt Jr. are high on his list of favorites. In all honesty, I doubt that he ever saw a driver that he didn't like. For that matter he has more friends among fellow NASCAR fans than anyone else could ever have. His Yeehawee fun luvin style has brought him that.

Even though he fancies himself as an old Kentucky hillbilly he has taught himself how to use Web TV and computers to become a major part of the online NASCAR discussion groups. Because of his vast knowledge and experience he now writes articles and stories for some of the better known Internet sites. His down home style and fun luvin nature are what make his stories different than most. When he's not tapping on that keyboard you'll find him yeehawin around the campgrounds at several different tracks in the Southeast having a great old time. That's everyones good buddy Omer...

YEEHAWEEING DOWN IN BRISTOL

Written by: Jim Johnson

This story is about the first time I met the author of this book, Omer Champion. But first I'll tell a little about myself. My name is Jim and I'm married to a wonderful lady named Rita. We live in Indiana and are big Dale Earnhardt fans. I started watching Nascar somewhere around 1984 and I've had it bad ever since.

The first race that we got to go to was Bristol in 1999. In November of 2000 we got a webtv. This was about the first time that I had been on the Internet and I didn't know jack about the net. It was cool because I could go to a lot of NASCAR and Earnhardt sites. Then one day I saw the word discuss and thought I'll check it out. I checked out a few discussion groups and then put in Nascar as the topic. For those of you that don't know what a discussion group is, it's a group that you can post a subject and other people can respond to it. Well, anyway I read some of the groups and started posting in one called this is ntmynic. The people in the group were real friendly and gave me a warm welcome.

In 2001, Omer posted about going to Bristol in March. I posted we were going. I got an email from Omer and he said that he would like to meet us. I email him back and said we would come and see him. He told me where he was camping so we could find him. He was only 1/2 mile down the road from where we were camping. We were really excited that we were going to meet Omer. We didn't know what we were getting into because there are a lot of crazy people out there, but we felt that Omer wasn't one of them. Rita and I started walking over to Omer's camp to meet him. Unsure of his campsite we began looking for the van with the 7 & 7 license plate on the front. We saw someone sitting at a table, and as we approached he stood up and yelled Yeehawee, I know you your Johnson3 (that was my name on webtv). We sat around and talked about Nascar and the people of the webtv group. He told us stories that I could only dream about.

On that day I made a friend that I will never forget. Now every year that we'll in Bristol we go over and see Omer. We have met some others from the webtv group too. NASCAR fans are the best.

In March of 2003 I wrote a song for Omer called YeeHaweeing down in Bristol. I play guitar so while we were there I sang the song to him and gave him a tape of it. If you ever get to meet Omer the first thing you will hear is YEEHAWEE. Thanks Omer for letting me tell my story. You are my Buddy.

By: Jeffery Dye

When it comes to racing, I think of racetracks, cars, drivers, and champions. The smell of the rubber and fuel burning as they race at an almost out of control speed, fenders banging, and paint swapping has become an addiction to many.

Racetracks are almost always exciting. They come in all sizes and shapes, offering many challenges. The tracks have been made out of dirt, asphalt, and concrete. The cars may race on all these, but the racing is different on each track because of these things. Short tracks offer tight racing with plenty of crashes, while super speedway tracks can have speeds so fast that the cars can look like a blur when they go by. The cars are the same way. Ford,

Chevy, Pontiac, Dodge, Plymouth, Mercury, and many others have raced over the years. Some were successful, while others were not. We can still see that today, with Pontiac leaving NASCAR after 2003, and the Dodge teams getting stronger.

The drivers are only alike in that they drive racecars. They come from the north, south, east, and west, where years ago most drivers came from only the south. Drivers have different styles of driving. Some are laid back just waiting for the right opportunity, while others seem that they can't wait that long. Champions have things in common such as accomplishing certain feats in their careers. The most common thing is consistency. That's what I can say about a champion I know personally.
He's been a consistent father, husband, friend, and race fan. It didn't matter to him if it was his "favorite driver" winning if the racing was good. He never really cared if it was a Dodge, Chevy, or Ford in front as long as he was watching what he loved to watch the most. Thank You Omer Champion, for being that "champion" that I know.

Jeffery Dye

SHORT "BIO" for Omer Champion

My name is Omer Champion. I was born at Seco, Kentucky on Sept. 3, 1938. Seco, Ky was a old coal mining camp where everyone in the community worked for "South East Coal Company". One of my grandfathers (Walter) was the first persons hired to take the first cut of coal for South East Coal Co. He was never able to attend school when he was a child because of poverty in his background. Everyone in his family had to work in order to survive. He was the father of 9 children and all of the men in his family became a employee of SECO.

A year later, my other grandfather (Bruce) also was employed by SECO. He had 5 children and his background was the same at Walter's. This was the beginning of several generations of my family to be involved in the mining of coal.

Some of the children never went to school, some went to the 3rd or 4th grade, but my dad managed to go to high school. Our family had a burning desire and high ambition to be successful through hard work and ambition.

Later on my dad managed to be one of the lucky one's of the family and went on to become a registered Mining Engineer. This is just a little background that will allow you to understand more about me and my future.

I was born at my grandmother's house at SECO. Even as a kid I was very ambitious because I had heard about the hard times that my family had suffered through. I just had the burning desire to be a success in life.

When I was 12 years old and in grade school, I started working for the people of my hometown. I delivered 3 different newspapers, cut grass, sold firewood, painted, planted trees and did any kind of work to make a dollar. It got to the point that everyone in the community wanted me to work for them. I was overwhelmed with so much work that it was not possible for me to do it all by myself.

My ambition took over and I decided that I would hire some of the other kids to work for me. I hired one at first, then two. Pretty soon it grew to six kids working for me. I was so proud of my little company which I had named "Omer's Work Crew". I continued working with this little company until I graduated from Fleming-Neon High School. In 1957 I graduated from high school and SECO gave me a full scholarship to the University of Kentucky to study Mining Engineering. I feel that my hard work, ambition and reputation as a child led to this scholarship. I became a mining engineer and a registered land surveyor. This gave me the opportunity to live my dreams which was to be self employed in a consulting engineering firm.

My dad and Chester Hooper had already formed a consulting engineering firm called H & C Contracting Engineers. Mr. Hooper wanted to retire and he sold his interest in the company to my dad. When I got out of college and decided to join my dad's business, we became partners, reorganized the business and changed the name to Champion Engineering Company. When my younger brother (Rick) graduated from the University of Kentucky he became a partner in our company.

Dad retired a few years later and I continued to manage the engineering firm for many years, until we sold the company and retired in 2000.

In 1964 I was married to Jo Crisp from Cleveland, TN. This was without a doubt the best blessing that I have ever received and I believe from the bottom of my heart that GOD sent her to me. She is a registered nurse and is working in the OR and will retire in Nov, 2004. We have been married 40 years and we are still like two little love birds, except our feathers are a little wrinkled. <smile>.

Jo and I have 3 grown children: Melody, is a registered nurse. Missy, is a certified school teacher and Champ(Omer, ll) is in the USAF training to become a F-16 fighter pilot. Champ will be graduating from the University of Kentucky in 2004 with a degree in electrical engineering.

Jo and I have 4 grandkids, Dylan, Cody, Sydney and Holly.

GOD has blessed me in so many ways that I could never ever give HIM all the praise that HE deserves. I am the happiest man on earth. I owe it all to GOD and my wife Jo. YEEE HAWEE !!! Omer

DEFINITION FOR YEEHAWEE

By: The Author, Omer Champion

Not many of you have heard the word YeeHawee because the Webster Dictionary doesn't list it. According to the dictionary this is not a word, but it is the word that I concocted myself. I am sure you may have heard the word HeeHaw from the old television show about 30 years ago. You also may be wondering why I am even dwelling to this and what it has to do with Nascar racing. Well my friend, it is hard to describe something that doesn't exist, but I will do the best I can in my old hillbilly way to describe it and tell you how it is connected with Nascar racing.

I have been going to Nascar races for 46 years beginning in 1958. During this time I have been camping at the races and I have met thousands of people and made friends with several fans that have camped with me every year. During the time we camped year after year together, we became very close friends and it just seemed that everyone was always happy and thrilled to be together. I for one, was one of the happiest fans and never held back my excitement and wanted to share it with everyone. When several of the others got happy you could hear them yell ALL RIGHT, OK, ATTA BOY, GO FOR IT and giving each other HIGH FIVE'S. There in lies the beginning of my concocted word "YeeHawee". I will try to give you some examples for my definition of YeeHawee. To me it means, happiness, togetherness, sharing, love, carefree, friendship, good times, closeness, no worries, no pressure, no depression, having a ball and being free. Now, there you have it as only a hillbilly like me could describe. It just so happened that the word YeeYawee became very popular and rubbed off on the rest of my friends as they all were yelling YeeHawee every time I met them. The word was common place at the campgrounds.

I would like to tell you a little story that illustrates how handy the word YeeHawee was for me and my friends one day at Talladega. Every year my friends and I would meet at the same place in the campground so that we could all camp together. We did this for about 20 years camping in the exact same spot. Camping was free at Talladega and it was on the first come first come basis. We would usually come to the campground on Thursday which would always give us time to claim our spot before the campground filled up. After camping at the same spot for about 20 years my son Champ and I went to Talladega. On the way down we just kept talking about had nice it was to be able to go to the race and was really looking forward to meeting our special friends that we had made over the years. Low and behold, when we got to the campground where we normally stay, we noticed a sign that said, NO CAMPING> THIS AREA RESERVED FOR PARKING. Gosh, what a awful feeling that was. It was like dropping a bomb shell on us. Sure, Talladega is a big place and has lots of room for campers. Well, that is true. However, our problem was not being able to locate our friends that we had camped with in the past. In case you are new to Talladega you need to understand that about 60,000 fans are camping and the camping covers about 600 acres. Hunting for our friends would be like hunting a certain grain of sand on Daytona Beach. Champ and I decided to sleep in the car as close as we could to the area where we camped, in hopes of seeing some of our friends. It was getting late and we had not seen anyone. We decided to go to sleep and see what we could do the next day to locate our friends.

We went to sleep in the car and the next morning about 6:00 am there was a pecking on my car window.

Gosh, I was so happy when I looked up as saw my old friend Bubby. Bubby always came with his dad, mother, Brian, Donald, Woodrow, Lula and sometimes others would come with them. Bubby told me where they were all camping, so I followed him and went to his new campsite. I knew we would never be able to get everyone back together again, but at least we now have a beginning for a new start. When I got to the campsite of Buddy's and met everyone we all started talking about how we would find all the others that we have been camping with. We had about 40 to 50 people that would camp with us year after year. After we talked for about a hour, my friend James, came up with a suggestion as to how we may find some of our friends. This brings us back to the beginning where we started with the description of YeeHawee.

It may be good for me to mention that every time I Yelled YeeHawee then others in our camp would yell YeeHawee back at me. James said, Omer you get in the back of my truck and I will drive you around and through all of the campgrounds while you keep yelling YeeHawee. That sound like a good idea and I felt like it would at least help us to find some of them.

Off we went in the truck. James was driving, his wife and Bubby was in the front seat and I was in the truck bed with about 6 other friends. As James started driving, we all started yelling YeeHawee. I am sure that everyone that we didn't know us thought we were crazy or at least drunk.

Well, that's ok with me because this idea worked great for us. When we started yelling YeeHaw, we could hear our friends yelling YeeHawee back to us. This had really made our day. We were able to find about 20 of them while making our rounds in the truck. They all broke camp where they were staying and followed us back to our campsite. We never found all of them, but we do have about 25 or 30 of us back together and we have made plans on how we will get back together if this happens again. Back then we didn't have the Internet with our addy's and all of the cell phones that we have today.

I hope you have enjoyed being in the YeeHawee school of learning and now know the definition to the word YeeHawee. If you ever come to Talladega, just look me up. all you have to do is yell YeeHawee and I will find you. Since you have been such a good student, I am sending you a special YeeHawee from me in the great state of Kentucky. YEEHAWEE. Omer

DONALD AND THE PORT-A-POTTY

I have attended every race at Talladega since the speedway opened in 1969. During this time I have seen so many funny, crazy, weird and sometimes even dangerous things happen. The story I am about to tell was funny, but it was also pitiful because it happened to one of my good friends named Donald.

When I go to Talladega I always camp with about 30 or 40 people that I have met from years past. Let me tell you now, camping is the only way to go if you want to have a good time which I call Good Time YeeHawee Style.

Now I will stop my babbling and get to the story. I was at Talladega in 1995 and the weather had been terrible from the time we got there on Thursday until about 2 hours before race time on Sunday. We could tell from the totally black sky that a real storm was coming. As a matter of fact it reminded me of the ingredients necessary for a tornado. Slowly it began to rain, but not hardly enough to get a person wet unless he stayed in the rain for a long time.

We were all sitting outside in our lawn chairs, just relaxing and sometimes telling a few jokes and lies. The weather began to get worse every minute and the rain started coming down much harder. One of my friends names Donald said that he wanted to go use the port-a-potty before it started raining harder. Donald left us and went to the port-a-potty which was about 100 yards away. The weather was at its worse now and the rain was coming down in sheets and the wind was blowing so hard that it was hard to stand up. Everyone started running to their tents, campers, truck, cars and motorhomes. I was camping in my tent, but when the weather ran us in, I decided to go with my friend James to his motorhome which would be more secure.

When I got to James motorhome, there were about 10 of us in it. The wind was blowing so bad, that it was almost blowing everything away in the campground. I saw my tent leave the ground, travel about 200 feet and then lodge against and around a tree. We could see everyone's canopies, tents, tables, chairs, stoves and almost anything you could mention; being blown away. We were witnessing what was almost a tornado.

After about 30 minutes, the storm let up and we had forgotten about Donald who went to the port-a-potty. My friend James asked me to go with him to check on Donald. When we got to where we could see, the port-a-potty was turned over and fell down with the front side where the door was on the ground. We could hear Donald inside kicking on the fiberglass. Since the door was on the bottom and against the ground, Donald was having a terrible time getting out. James and I managed to use some large rocks, stick and a hunting knife to break loose the top while Donald was inside kicking the top. Finally, the top broke loose and we were able to let Donald crawl out.

I just don't think is is possible to describe in words what a funny site it was to see Donald completely covered with sewage and at the same time we were trying not to laugh so that we would not embarrass him. Donald was a total mess. As a matter of fact he was destroyed.

The campground has no water and what were we going to do to help Donald clean up and get rid of that stinky smell? One of our friends came up with a good idea. He said there was a car wash about 5 miles from us on the way to Oxford. We loaded Donald in the back of a pick up truck and hauled him to the car wash. When we got there we put money into the slot and started spraying him with the high pressure was wands. That did the trick and we had Donald clean and good as new. Donald went into the restroom at the car wash and changed clothes.

On the way back to the campground Donald started laughing so much that he was cackling out loud, I think he was so glad that it was over that he was almost ready to shout. I also realize, this story may be hard to believe, but let me tell you that it is the honest truth. However, I do know it was a little S____Y.

YEEHAWEE to my good buddy Donald!

JO AND THE KFC BUCKET

Long before I got married I was a race fan. The first race I went to was in 1958. I got married to Jo in January, 1964. We went to Miami FL on our honeymoon. While driving to Miami, I drove by Daytona International Speedway just to show Jo the track and surrounding area. Little did she know at the time that she would be going to the Firecracker 250 on the 4th of July. Jo had little or no knowledge of racing but tried to show some interest to make me happy.

When we got back home to Kentucky, I immediately made all of the reservations and arrangements for us to be able to attend the race on the 4th of July. We had a room reserved at the Holiday Inn on the beach and near the Boardwalk. This would make for a great vacation for both of us. Jo loves the beach and loves to go shopping. My fun was being able to go to the racing events at the speedway. I was so excited and couldn't hardly wait for our first July vacation. July finally came and we headed out to Daytona Beach and checked into the Holiday Inn. We were there several days before the race and I made sure that Jo was able to do what ever made her happy at the time. I was looking forward to seeing the Paul Revere 250 and the Firecracker 250.

When it came time to go to the race, we stopped by a Kentucky Fried Chicken and bought a bucket of Chicken to take to the race. It was about 8:00 pm when we got to the race track. This time factor may sound odd to some of you younger race fans, but for your benefit, please let me explain the schedule and format for the race. The Paul Revere 250 was a race for sports car on the road course and the race would start a midnight. That is why it is called the Midnight Ride of Paul Revere. There were no lights at Daytona at this time and the cars had headlights and brake lights. The race was scheduled for midnight and it was schedule to end at 3:00 am regardless of how many laps had been run. The Firecracker 250 was scheduled to start the next morning at 10:00 am in order to be finished before the sun got so hot and also to allow the fan to enjoy the rest of the day at the beach. Jo and I went inside the speedway at about 9:00 pm which gave us lots of time to walk about, look at the car, shops and just enjoy our time together.

When the race started Jo seemed to enjoy it, but after a few lap, I noticed that she was getting a little sleepy; maybe due to being bored. When the race was over and we were walking back to the car, I was dreading the drive back to the motel and because the traffic was so bad I knew it would be about 6:00 am before we got to the motel and we would have to leave about 8:00 am in order to get back to the Firecracker race. I told Jo that we would just sleep in the car and avoid all the hassle with the traffic. Jo agreed, and everything was going well until she said I need to go to the bathroom to pee. Low and behold, there was no bathroom in sight and the speedway was locked tight. For a man this would not be much of a

24

problem, we could go behind a car, tree, bush or almost anywhere to pee. However, it is not that simple for a woman.

Well, I came up with the bright idea the we still had the KFC bucket in the car. I asked Jo to use the KFC bucket. She said she was afraid the someone would look through the window and see her. She also had another problem. She was afraid the buck would turn over and spill in the car. I knew she had no choice and I encouraged her to use the KFC bucket. I held the bucket while she relieved herself. When she finished, she made sure that I was the one to go out and empty the bucket. There I went carrying the bucket to find a good place to pour it out. What a sight that must have been. We went to the Firecracker race and I loved every minute of it, but poor old Jo was so tired from staying up most of the time that she went to sleep with all that noise. That is one good sign of being totally exhausted. I kept trying to wake her up, but she kept going back to sleep.

Finally, I looked at her and said, "Wake up Colonel Sanders, everyone will think you are drunk". All in all, it turned out to be a great vacation for both of us, but you can bet that we didn't stop at KFC on the way back to Kentucky.

WHO DO YOU THINK YOU ARE? Richard Petty

Back when Nascar was first organized in 1948 almost all of the races were held in the south. As the sport grew and Nascar started expanding to other parts of the country several new tracks were built. One of the new expansion tracks that was built was at Dover, DE. The race track at Dover had a horse racing track inside of the stock car track. That is where Dover got the name of Dover Downs. This was a very beautiful track which was highly banked and was one mile in length. When the first race was scheduled at Dover, Richard Petty was one of the most popular drivers on the circuit, but maybe not as well known up north as he was in the south. Now days the driver all fly to the tracks or travel in an escorted motor home with the most modern conveniences. On one day in particular, Richard Petty was driving to Dover. He was cruising along on the highway when all of a sudden he looked in his rear view mirror and saw the flashing light and heard the siren of a police officer. Richard carefully pulled over to the shoulder of the road and stopped. The policeman came up to his car carrying his citation book and walked up to passenger side of the car. The policeman told Richard that he was driving beyond the speed limit and was going to have to give him a ticket. The policeman had no idea who Richard was. The policeman had heard the name of Richard Petty, but due to being up north, he had no idea what Richard looked liked and sure didn't know he was talking to the man himself. The policeman said, Who do you thing you are Richard Petty? Richard, was so polite to the policeman and while flashing that familiar smile, Richard said yes, I am Richard Petty. What a surprise that was for the policeman. Richard showed the policeman his driver's license and that sure made the policeman excited. He could not believe that he had met the greatest stock car driver of his time. Richard thanked the policeman for doing his job and the policeman got Richard's autograph. However, here are the big question? Did the policeman give him a ticket? Did the policeman get his autograph on a regular piece of paper or did the policeman keep the ticket to use as a autograph? I would like to know the answer to those questions. If anyone ever finds out this answer, please share it with me, because I am not sure what the true answer would be.

However, I do know that Richard is a gentlemen and I also know that the policeman will remember that day for the rest of his life.

BENNY PARSONS AND THE HOT DOG.

Today Benny Parsons is associated with a tv network and does a great job in his relatively new profession. When I first met Benny Parsons he was a very young, tall and slim trimmed man that was driving in the ARCA division of motor racing. Today Benny has changed a lot and he is now known as Buffet Benny. I have always like and respected Benny. He was a very good driver and one that most call a perfect gentlemen. It was so hard to find any fan that didn't like him. He was so good to the fans and always took time to share with them. I will never for the first time I met him and that meeting will remain in my mind as one of the highlights of my racing life. I love the story that follows and today, I even enjoy it more because this happened about 35 years ago. I went to a ARCA race at Bristol in the late 60's. Benny was driving a yellow and white #98 Ford which was owned by Harry Ranier. Back in those days the fans were allowed in the pits before and after the race to mix and mingle with the drivers and crews. I was in the pit on that day and had to be back at my seat two hours before the race started. It was almost time for the announcement to be made, that everyone must return to their seats. How luck I was. All of a sudden it started to rain very hard and I knew the race would be delayed several hours. This made me so happy, because it would give me all the time I wanted to talk to the drivers. I decided to go to the concession stand to buy a hot dog and Coke before trying to talk to the drivers. When I got back from the concession stand, I saw Benny and one of his crew members standing under a umbrella. I walked up to them, said hello and they were very courteous and started to talk to me. When Benny saw my hot dog, he said I am starved to death. Where did you get that hot dog? I asked him did he want me to get one for him and his friend. He said yes, but I don't have any money because my driving suit has no pockets. That made me happy to hear this because I would consider it an honor to buy a hot dog for Benny Parsons. His friend didn't want one, so I headed out to buy a hot dog and Coke for Benny. I came back with the hot dog and Coke and I saw a third party standing there with him. I gave him the hot dog and coke. He introduced me to the third person. Who was that person? That third person just happened to be his wife. Benny took one bite of the hot dog and then his wife reached out, grabbed the hot dog and started eating it. She ate the whole hot dog and poor old Benny was left to starve to death. Do you think that might be why old Benny eats so much today and has the nickname Buffet Benny? Since that day, I have met Benny many times and I still admire him as much and probably more than I did the first day I met him at Bristol. Several years has passed since that blessed day in my life and Benny had a live talk show on the radio in 1999. I was listening to his program one night and someone called in to ask him a question. Benny said that he was not sure of that answer and that he would try to find out the correct answer and reveal it later in the program. That question caused me to sit up and pay attention, because I knew the answer to the question that the fan had asked. I called the number to his live radio program and was soon connected live to Benny. I told Benny the answer to the question and he said, yes that is correct, I remember it now. I then decided to ask him a question and he said go for it. I said Benny, do you remember someone buying you a hot dog and Coke at Bristol about 30 years ago?

You should have heard the excitement in his voice when he said, I sure do, but my wife ate every bite of it. Now that deserves a big YeeHawee. What a story that was and how precious the memory is to me. Forever, I will never forget Benny Parsons,the hot dog and Coke.

TIME FLOCK and JOCKO FLOCKO

I have been writing and telling the story for many years about Tim Flock and his monkey Jocko Flocko. This is one of the best stories that you will ever hear about Nascar racing. I have always enjoyed telling this story in my own words based on the way I read it in the media. Most of the time when I have told this story is was just a short version of what I had heard many times in the past. I have read many articles about Tim Flock and his monkey Jocko Flock, but the best I have ever seen it written was by Michael Smith. Thanks to Michael I will be able to share this story with you.

By Michael Smith

It's safe to say that Tim Flock is the only NASCAR driver who ever lost a race because of a monkey. The episode happened during the 1950's and the monkey was a passenger in Flock's car, but we're getting ahead of the story.

Tim Flock along with his three older brothers Carl, Bob and Fonty, grew up in Fort Payne, Alabama during the tough years of the Great Depression. Tim's father passed away in 1925 on the eve of the national economic collapse and the family struggled to make ends meet. To supplement the family income, the three older Flock brothers assisted their uncle Peachtree Williams in his moonshine business, making two runs a day to Dahlonega, Georgia. It wasn't long before the youngest Flock boy was riding along on the delivery excursions as well. Naturally, as is the case whenever youngsters gather with fast cars, the Flocks eventually got around to running their car against other 'shine runners to see whose cars were fastest on a given day. As with the day-to-day running of moonshine, young Tim Flock tagged along when the racing competitions were held, too. Bob and Fonty got the jump on younger Tim, though Tim would rise to greater prominence in what came to be NASCAR. Bob and Fonty participated in some of the earliest stock car showdowns in the 1930s, running primarily at Dawsonville, Georgia. Tim jumped into the fray a bit later, in 1947 to be exact and later that year he claimed his first win at Lakewood Speedway in Atlanta. When Big Bill France ran an experimental NASCAR event in February of 1949 it was Bob Flock who claimed the checkered flag and within months, France held the first "Strictly Stock" (what is today known as Winston Cup) race at Charlotte, North Carolina and the three Flock brothers were in the field when the green flag dropped. At the end of the day Fonty finished second behind the wheel of a '49 Hudson, young Tim finished fifth driving an Olds 88 and Bob, who started from the pole, finished thirty-second due to an engine failure in his '46 Hudson. Tim's first NASCAR victory came the following year when he bested his own brother Bob to win the second Grand National event at Charlotte. Of the three racing Flock brothers, Tim would go on to have the best career as a driver, despite the fact that his career was cut short by forces outside his control.

Tim captured his first national championship in 1952 driving Hudson Hornet's for Ted Chester, an Atlanta car dealer. With a flat head straight-six engine, the Hornet would seem an unlikely candidate for stock car racing dominance. Even when fitted with a specially designed racing carburetor, the Hornet produced only in the neighborhood of 170 horsepower. The secret to the Hudson Hornet's success was the fact that in NASCAR's formative years, many races were still run on dirt and the Hornet's low revving torque made it a killer on dirt tracks.

On the way to the 1952 championship, Tim Flock won 8 times and finished in the top five no less than 14 times. The next two years Flock's on-track performance tapered off a great deal and he posted just a single victory in 1953 and no victories in 1954. It should be pointed out that Flock ran only five races in 1954, after quitting in disgust after having the Daytona victory taken away from him by Big Bill France.

A post race inspection found polished ports in the carburetor and the victory was taken away. Flock vowed never to race in NASCAR again.

Tim Flock opened a Pure Oil station in Atlanta and seemed content to live out his life as an entrepreneur, were it not for a fortuitous twist of fate. When the 1955 Daytona race rolled around, Flock had no intention of attending the event even as a spectator much less as a competitor until a group of his buddies showed up and convinced him to travel to Florida to take in race festivities.

Once there, Flock and his buddies stood watching the time trials one day during Speedweeks as a Chrysler 300 roared by on the wide flat beach. Out loud Flock said if he had a car like that under him, he could win the race. Well, unbeknownst to Flock a local Mercury Outboard Motors dealer overheard the remark and recognized Flock as the previous year's disqualified winner. The dealer introduced Flock to the owner of the Chrysler 300 team, Carl Kiekhaefer who was NASCAR's first big time multi-car team owner and as luck would have it, Kiekhaefer was looking for another driver.

Flock stepped into one of Kiekhaefer's Chrysler's and took the pole for the Daytona beach race, then finished second behind Fireball Roberts on race day. Ironically, the following day, while eating breakfast, Flock and Kiekhaefer were informed that Roberts' car had been disqualified for having illegal engine components, so the victory was given to Flock. Tim Flock remained with the Kiekhaefer team for the remainder of the 1955 season and enjoyed phenomenal success, winning a record 18 races in 39 starts. Life as a Kiekhaefer team driver had its bonuses and its drawbacks. As the inventor of the Mercury outboard motor, Carl Kiekhaefer was interested primarily in gaining publicity for his team and his product. To Kiekhaefer, already a wealthy man, the prize money was secondary at best. Flock received a monthly salary of $2,500 and he was allowed to keep all the prize money from his races.

Additionally, Kiekhaefer occasionally paid a bonus for races won during the season. But the benefits did not come without sacrifice. Kiekhaefer ruled the team with an iron fist, insisting on a strict curfew and rigid sleeping arrangements while on the road, even for the married drivers. During test runs and qualifying, drivers were required to monitor engine gauges and were debriefed afterward, much like military pilots following missions. The strict regimentation grated on the free spirited Flock and, when Kiekhaefer began choosing which driver would win certain races, ordering the others to pit during green flag laps, Flock had had enough. Flock resigned from the team in early 1956 but not before claiming his second championship with a stellar run in 1955. His single season win record of 18 victories would stand until Richard Petty's outstanding 1967 season.

Flock ran fourteen more races during the 1956 season, his final victory coming in Bill Stroppe's M335 Mercury at Elkhart Lake. He continued to race on into the 1961 season but the past success was never matched and that year he ran afoul of Big Bill France when he, along with Curtis Turner, attempted to organize NASCAR drivers into a union. Turner had gotten into financial trouble in his efforts to build Charlotte Motor Speedway. In an effort to raise money Turner approached teamster's boss Jimmy Hoffa who offered to help monetarily in exchange for Turner's promise to organize NASCAR's drivers. Tim Flock, who had butted heads with Big Bill France many times in the past, joined Turner in his effort and, when the whole organizing plan fell apart, both Turner and Flock received lifetime bans from NASCAR racing.

In 1966, with the manufacturers pulling out of the sport, Big Bill France was forced to lift the ban in order to get the former big name drivers back into the fold. Turner accepted the offer but years of battling Big Bill France had left Tim Flock justifiably tired and bitter and he adamantly refused to return to racing cars. Flock did continue to work in the ranks of NASCAR, primarily as program director at Charlotte Motor Speedway until retiring in the Charlotte area.

During the 1998 celebration of NASCAR's 50th Anniversary, Tim Flock received some measure of the recognition he deserved. Numerous media outlets interviewed Flock and Darrell Waltrip ran a special all-white paint scheme with Flock's trademark number 300 during qualifying for one race. (NASCAR got the last word in, however, by refusing the number 300 to run during the race due to the potential for scoring problems with a 3-digit number on the car. Waltrip ran the paint scheme with his customary number 17 instead. To some, it represented NASCAR's final swipe at a once great driver.) Sadly, while at the height of the sport's celebration, Tim Flock was diagnosed with cancer and did not live out the season, though he departed the worldly ranks of racing full in the knowledge that he was well respected and recognized for his contribution to American stock car racing.

But what about the monkey you ask? In 1953, during Tim Flock's tenure with the Ted Chester racing team, Mr. Chester decided it would be a neat gimmick to have a rhesus monkey ride along with Flock in the car during races. A small raised seat was constructed on the passenger side of the racecar and little "Jocko Flocko" as he came to be called, was outfitted with a miniature driving suit. The setup was a success and fans apparently delighted in seeing the little monkey whizzing past during races, but on May 30, 1953 things got out of hand. During a race Jocko got loose from his seat and proceeded to climb around inside the racecar. In those days, many of the cars in NASCAR racing were equipped with a trap door on the passenger side floorboard. During races a driver could lift open the trapdoor to check the wear on his right front tire. Well, Jocko was evidently an observant little fellow and, having seen Tim lift the trapdoor numerous times during previous races, he decided to lift the door and have a look for himself.

What happened next is unclear; either Jocko got too close to the spinning tire and skinned himself, or a rock flew up and hit him. Whatever the cause, the result is undisputed; Jocko went berserk and began tearing around inside the car. Tim found himself forced to restrain his "co-driver" with one hand while steering for the pits with the other. Thus, a first place finish turned into a third place finish, and all because of a monkey.

RICHARD PETTY AND MY RACING JACKET

In 1967 I purchased a Union 76 Jacket that had lots of Richard Petty patches on it. I loved that jacket so much and I took it to every race that I went to and hoped that someday I would be able to get Richard to autograph it. That day finally came and here is the story about the day Richard Petty autographed my Jacket. The greatest and most exciting day of my racing life was in 1970 when I was staying at a motel in Anniston AL. It was the weekend of the Talladega race. My room was on the second floor overlooking the swimming pool. I was sitting at a table near the window in my room. When I looked out the window, low and behold, who did I see? I could not believe it, but it was Richard Petty.

Richard was sitting on top of a rock wall that surrounded the swimming pool. There were several people in the swimming pool, but Richard was sitting on the wall and no one was around him. I knew this would be the best chance I would ever have to get my jacket autographed by Richard. I walked down to the pool, knowing that Richard was probably trying to relax and I sure didn't want to be the one to interrupt his quiet time.

I had seen and talked to Richard many times, but it was always in the presence of other fans. This would be a very special time for me because I would be able to talk with him on a more personal basis. I walked up to Richard and extended my hand for a hand shake and he shook hand while flashing that famous Petty smile. This was such a special occasion for me. I told him about the jacket that I had bought and asked him to autograph it. He seemed so happy to do this for me. As I stood there watching him sign the jacket, I was just think about how great he was as a driver and a person. When he finished signing the jacket, I thanked him and told him that I wanted to respect his quiet time and I started to walk away. Richard said in paraphrase, stick around awhile if you want to. I am just waiting for my family and the boys (his crew) to be here. Gosh, I like to died with excitement. I hopped up on that wall, sit down and started talking with him. Naturally, it seemed that his racing career would get top priority during our conversation, but what a surprise I got, when he kept asking me questions about myself and seemed more interested in talking about my life. I was shocked, but happy. After about 30 minutes of being with Richard a 12 passenger Petty blue van pulled up in the parking lot. The van was driven by Dale Inman who was Richard's crew chief. When the van unloaded, there stood Lee, Elizabeth, Lynda, Maurice, Kyle, Sharon and Wade Thornburg. I was able to say hello to all of them, but in the back of my mind the thought was still there telling me to respect them and call it a day. What a great day this was to be in the mist of so many people that I have admired for years.

I thanked Richard for allowing me to spend the time with him and I started back to my room. On the way back to my room, tears of joy came to my eyes as I counted my blessing for such a wonderful day in my life.

Richard Petty has been, is now and always will be the number one hero and role model in my life. He has a personality of gold that will make you feel more important than he is.

DAVID PEARSON AND THE CIGARETTES

In my opinion David Pearson was one of the greatest drivers in the history of stock car racing. He finished second on the all time win list to Richard Petty, but you must consider that David didn't run as many races as Richard. Every time I see or hear the name of David

Pearson, it reminds me of a day that my brother Rick and I was able to talk to him in the pits at Bristol. Here is the story about David Pearson and his homemade cigarette holder.

In 1968 my brother Rick and I went to the race at Bristol. At that time we had more freedom of access to the drivers than we have today. David Pearson was driving the blue and gold #17 Ford which was owned by Holman and Moody. David was sitting in his car just on the inside of pit wall when Rick and I walked up to talk with him. We could see that David was having some type of problem with his eye. He kept rubbing his eye and he told us that he had some foreign object in his eye. I suggested to David that he let me look into the eye and see what the problem was. He agreed. When I gently pulled up his eyelid, I could see a small black particle in his eye. I took a corner of a small cloth, rolled it up to use as a tool to lift the object out of his eye. When I got it out, David said that sure feels better.

During the time that I was trying to play doctor with David, my brother Rick had noticed a homemade cigarette holder attached to the dashboard inside his car. I looked at the cigarette holder and was surprised to see it in the car. The holder was made from a small piece of plywood. It had holes drilled in it with the same diameter as the cigarettes. David would stand up the cigarettes in the holder which would allow him to have one without having to fumble around for a cigarette. David told Rick and I that it was hard for him to drive the car for 500 laps without a cigarette and that was the purpose of having the holder in his car.

This is a good example of how things have changed in the racing world today. Can you imagine what the sanctioning body would do if they saw that homemade cigarette holder in one of the high tech cars of today?

CALE YARBOROUGH TAKING HOSE BATH

Cale Yarborough was one of the toughest and meanest racers of all times. He believed in running every lap flat out. as if it was the final lap. I have seen Cale race so many times and I will have to agree that he is one of the sports greatest chargers.

In July of 1968 I attended the race at Bristol. It was so hot that day that the oil was seeping out of the asphalt. You must remember that in 1968 the cars had no power steering and no window vents to let in some much need fresh air. It was a gruesome day for all of the drivers and some of them were not able to go the distance and had to be replaced by other drivers that had fallen out of the race or did not make the starting lineup. So many drivers became exhausted by heat that there were no drivers left to relief drive for them. Those drivers had to park the car behind the wall and call it quits for the day.

Cale was one of the tougher drivers and finally finished the 500 laps. He was driving for the Wood Brothers in the #21 Mercury Cyclone. After the race was over, my brother Rick and I were one of the first groups of fans allowed in the pit area. When we got to the pit area we found Cale still sitting in his car and he looked like someone that was ready to be taken to the emergency room. He was so tired that he could not remove his helmet. Leonard, Glen and Eddie Wood came to the car and had to physically life him out and let him lay on the ground. The rescue squad came by and gave him some oxygen until he started breathing normally again.

After the rescue squad left the Wood Brothers carried him to a folding lawn chair and they used a pressurized water hose to spray him down. The hose bath lasted for about 15 minutes and then Cale begin to smile and start talking. When he started talking I was able to talk with him. I told him that I knew he was tough and would be one of those to finish the race. He said he thought he was tough and was doing alright when he was totally concentration on his driving, but when the race was over he just gave up and then the heat like to killed him. Finally, Cale's wife Betty Jo came to the scene and she started laughing, kidding and making jokes at Cale's expense. That made Cale get well in a hurry. Cale was himself again and told Betty Jo that she would have to do the driving back to South Carolina.

We sure have come a long ways since 1968. Now days, all a driver has to do is be able to walk back to his $500,000.00 air conditioned motor home. I am sure if Cale was driving today he would appreciate that kind of motor home.

MY 5 ALL TIME WORSE RACING MEMORIES

Listed below are the 5 WORSE memories that I have relating to me being a Nascar fan for 45 years.

1 My number one racing buddy was named James Willis who lived in Tuscumbia, AL. I met James, his wife Clara, his son James Jr. and his son Brian for the first time at Talladega in 1970. As I do with most of my racing friends, I gave James a nickname "Alabama Wildman". We all camped together twice each year at Talladega for 28 years which would be a total of 56 times. During this time we felt like we were family and not just friends. The last time I camped with him was at Talladega and he told me that he was going to the race at Atlanta in November and asked me to meet him and his family there and camp with them. I agreed to meet him at Atlanta and that was the last time I ever saw James. We went our separate ways and on Nov 12, 1998 I was at my home and James called me the day before we were to leave for Atlanta. He

said, I am getting ready to go to the store to buy groceries for Atlanta and I will meet you at the campground tomorrow at 4pm. As usual, before he hangs up the phone, he would always call me some awful name that only a friend would do. Four hours later, the phone rang again and it was his wife Clara. Clara said, "Omer, James went to the grocery store and on his way back home he was killed in his truck when a train hit him." I was hurt so bad, that I couldn't talk and Clara was not able to talk any more, so she just hung up the phone. That was the most horrible day of my racing life. I still camp with his family, but the heart of our family is no longer with us, but will be in my heart and memory forever.

2 The first race I went to was at Darlington in 1958. It sure didn't take me long to determine who my favorite driver would be. I had listen to some of the races on the radio and read a lot about them in newspapers and I kept hearing about Fireball Roberts. Naturally, when I got to the track his car was the first one I started looking for. When I found his car, Fireball was sitting on the pavement and leaning with his back against the car. I was magic as if I was watching Superman or Roy Rogers. I began to look at all of the car and trying to determine who each driver was, but my eyes and mind kept coming back to Fireball and the #22 car. Yes, that was the day I became a Fireball Roberts fan. I went to several races after that, but let me tell you, that guy was one awesome driver. I went to three more races that year and in 1959 I went to the very first Daytona 500 along with 12 other races. By the time 1964 had rolled around, I was married and my business was well established and I was going to 18 races each year. In May of 1964, I went to the World 600 at Charlotte and didn't know at that time how terrible this day would be for me. You all know the story about the wreck between Ned Jarrett, Junior Johnson and

Fireball, so I will not tell that story again. When that wreck occurred it was so horrible for me to stand there and watch my hero burning to death while Ned and Junior were trying to free him from the fire. Had it not been for Ned and Junior, Fireball would have died in his car. I went to the Firecracker race at Daytona which was scheduled for the 4th of July. I was there on the 2nd of July watching practice when Nascar threw the red flag, asked all drivers to return to the pit and requested that everyone stand for the following announcement. The announcer said, "Ladies and Gentlemen, the Great Fireball has died". That broke my heart and I cried like a baby. Ironically this was on Richard Petty's birthday and that was the day I first became a Richard Petty fan.

3 My next worse memory is one that all of you are familiar with, therefore I will not get into this story, but it was the day that Dale Earnhardt was killed. We lost a big part of racing on that day and that void will remain with us for the rest of our lives.

4 Alabama International Motor Speedway as it was called back then had its first race in 1969. Being an engineer and a race fan, I was not only interested in the racing, but I had a very big interest in wanting to see some of the construction that was taking place in that Magic Kingdom (that is what I called it). I took 3 of my employees with me and we went to Talladega to watch some of the construction. I was granted permission to be there via phone call to Don Nanman. We watched the construction for two days and I was like a little kid looking for Santa Claus, because I knew when the first race was held that I would be there. This upcoming race, was without a doubt the most I have ever looked forward to seeing. I simply was counting down the days and getting excited for that day to finally come. Well, that day finally did come, but it turned out to be one of the worse

days of my racing life. The day before the race the drivers formed a union called the Professional Drivers Association and elected Richard Petty as president of the PDA. The PDA formed a boycott and decided not to race because they didn't think the tires were good enough to withstand the high speeds and also other safety reasons. Bill France, Sr. said the track was safe and he would prove it by driving a car himself around the speedway. Big Bill, used someone's back up car and drove it around 190 (?) miles per hour. The boycott was not lifted, but Big Bill was determined to have that race and decided to make this deal with the fans and any driver that would enter. At that time the WC was called GN. The Busch Series was called Sportsmen and there was another division that was call GT. Big Bill told all drivers of all divisions that if they would race, he would combine all cars and the purse for the race would be the same as posted for the big boys. Man, this went over like gang busters. This was a chance for the underdogs to make some big money for a change. About 10 of the independent drivers broke rank and decided to race, but only one top rated driver, Bobby Isaac joined them. The fans could use their ticket and see the race or get a refund in full. This being the first race (most tickets being sold at the gate) no one knew for sure how many fans would be there, but I was announced that about 80 percent chose to see the race. The race sure was different and was lots of fun to watch and sometimes it was even comical. The race was won by RICHARD BRICKHOUSE, in the #99 Dodge Daytona owned by Ray Nichols and was suppose to be driven by Charlie Glotzbach. I am glad that I chose to stay and see the race, but this was not what I came to see. I came to see Richard, Cale, David, Buddy, Charlie, Bobby, Donnie and all of the top dogs. For that reason, this is one of my WORSE racing memories.

5 This is also one that everyone is familiar with and I am sure you will be happy to know that I will not be going into details. When Dale Earnhardt, Sr. wrecked Terry Labonte at Bristol, it almost made me sick to my stomach. Dale was my favorite driver, but doing this to Terry was hard for me to take.

MY 5 ALL TIME BEST RACING MEMORIES

Here are my 5 all time BEST Nascar memories during my 45 years as a race fan.

1 In 1970 I went to a race at Talladega and I was staying at a motel in Anniston, AL. I was in my room sitting at a table and looked out of the window and saw Richard Petty sitting up on a rock wall that surrounded the swimming pool. Richard was alone. I had just bought a Richard Petty jacket and had been carrying it to the races trying to get it autographed by Richard. I went down to the swimming pool and asked him to sign my jacket. I thanked him and told him that I didn't won't to invade his privacy and started to leave. He said, just hang around, I am sitting here waiting for my family to arrive in a few minutes. I was able to talked to Richard one on one for about 30 minutes. Soon a Petty Blue 12 passenger van pulled up and was driven by Dale Inman, his crew chief. When everyone unloaded from the van it was Lee, Elizabeth, Lynda, Kyle, Sharon, Maurice, Wade Thornbury and others. I said hello to them and left with tears in my eyes from counting my blessings.

2 In the early 70's I went to a race at Rockingham. The race was rained out. I would be going by Richard's old homeplace and garage on my way home. I knew Richard would be coming there and I took off the make sure I was there when he came home. When I got to Lee's house which was the house that Richard was born in, I

saw Lee sitting on the porch. I walked up to him and told him I was waiting for Richard to come home and would go sit in my car to wait on him. It was raining and Lee said just come up here and sit down and wait for Richard. I came up on the porch and he told me to sit in that rocking chair over there. I sit down and he started telling me about the rocking chair and I could see that the rocking chair was very important to him. Lee told me that his daddy made that chair when he (Lee) was 12 years old. Never in my lifetime would I ever thought that I would be sitting in a chair that was hand made for Richard Petty's Grandfather. When Richard came to the shop he was with about 10 of his crew members and Richard let me go into the shop and watch the crew unload the car and tools. OH, what I would give to own that old rocking chair.

3 My brother Rick and I was going to the race at N. Wilksboro. We passed a motel and Rick saw Cale Yarborough coming out of his room and we pulled into the parking lot. We started talking to Cale and he was so nice and friendly to us. During our conversation, Cale said he was waiting for a police escort to the track. Cale had a rental car. I told Cale, it must be nice to be able to miss all of that traffic and be escorted. Two police cars pulled into the parking lot and Cale said if you want to you can go with me until we start to turn into the track.
Man, I would have gone with him to DETROIT CITY. Cale told the police that I was going with them. In front was a police car, next was Cale, then me and then a police car bringing up he rear. I will remember that day forever. My brother and I still talk about this every time we are together.

4 Back in the older days, the drivers cars were pulled behind a truck on a open trailer. I had gone to the (year?) Daytona 500 and was driving up South Atlantic Ave when

I saw Bobby Allison and his Coca Cola car sitting in the parking lot of the SEA DIP motel. Bobby, Donnie, Eddie and several others were working on the car in the parking lot. They had no problem with me coming up to watch them work on the car. Can you imagine that happening today? No way.

5 One time in the 60's I went to a race at Charlotte and was staying at the Holiday Inn on Tryon Street. I walked down to the lounge and I saw Buck Baker, Smokey Yunick and Louise Smith sitting at a table near the dance floor. For those of you that may not know, Louise Smith was a race driver. It was early in the afternoon and there wasn't very many people in the lounge. I decided to walk over and speak to them, but much to my surprise Buck asked me to sit down. That sure made me a happy camper. I sit and talked to them about 45 minutes. IT'S FIVE O'CLOCK SOMEWHERE.

SHORTY, THE PYROTECH KID

Sometime during the 70's I went to the race at Darlington with my brother Rick and our friend Johnny. We arrived at Darlington Friday afternoon about 6:00 pm and started trying to find a good camping site. We finally located a good spot to pitch our tent. There was another tent already there near where we pitched our tent. After we got our camp set up we built a campfire and it was just beginning to get dark. Some of the race fans had started to shoot some fireworks and we were enjoying sitting around, relaxing and watching the fireworks. After about a hour, we could see someone coming out of the tent that was next to ours. Now, I am no big man by any means, but the guy crawling out of that tent was a very small person that made me feel like a giant.

He was so dirty, rugged and looked like he had just crawled out of a ditch. He finally got out of the tent, but he seemed so weak that he could barely stand up. He was not drunk, but probably had just woke up with a hangover. He made his way over to our campfire and told us his name was Shorty. I told him he was welcome to sit around our campfire with us. That seem to make he feel welcome. I knew then that his problem was the hangover. Everyone seems to tell you what to do, eat or drink to get over the hangover. In my opinion, there is no cure for a hangover. Excessive alcohol in one's system depletes the sugar in the body and the hangover will last until the body replenishes the sugar. Even though I don't believe there is a cure, I just tried to make Shorty feel better by giving him some candy to eat.

As we sit around the campfire, we were getting to know each other very well. Shorty, seemed to be a very nice guy. He was very friendly and enjoyed talking. We all liked him but he seem to have one big hang up on fireworks. It seem that he wanted to talk about fireworks all the time. It didn't matter what anyone said, the conversation came back to fireworks. Shorty started telling us about how many fireworks and fireworks accessories he had in the back of his truck that had a camper top. He took us over the the truck and It would be impossible for me to tell you what he had in that truck. He had every fireworks imaginable and so many accessories to use with the fireworks. He had homemade guns that he used to shoot the fireworks from. He has special made racks, tubes, conduit, barrels and almost everything you could imagine that could be associated with fireworks. We were camping underneath some huge trees where there were only small openings above where you could see the sky. Shorty got busy shooting his fireworks and it was amazing to watch him and see how excited he got. He was just like a kid that had just seen Santa Claus. Shorty, would use some of his homemade accessories and would put every firework through the small openings in the trees. We were all amazed at what we were seeing. After shooting fireworks for about 3 hours Shorty said, you haven't seen anything you. He said, just wait to tomorrow night and I will show everyone that I am the best in the business when it comes to fireworks. I told him I was so impressed, that I was going to give him another nickname which would be the Pyrotech Kid. For the rest of the trip we all started calling him the Pyrotech Kid.

When the next night came on us, Shorty walked over to our campfire and said, boys tonight is the night and I will have the biggest fireworks show that you will ever see. Man, was he ever right? That man shot everything you could imagine for a total of 3 hours. Then, he told us that it was time for the grand finale. He took a gallon paint can, filled it half full with carbide, added some aluminum, a cup of water and drilled a small hole in the bottom of the can. When that mixture started to react, he put the lid on the can and tapped the lid to make it secure. He laid the can down on its side, stood back about 30 feet and used a homemade devise to shoot a lighted tracer directly at the hole he had drilled in the can. When that can exploded, it was a sight to see. The explosion was so loud that it sounded like a ton of dynamite had been ignited.

It always seems that some bad comes when everyone is having a good time doing things that they should not do. The explosion blew Shorty's tent down and totally ripped it in shreds. We also had a visit from the Sheriff's department. Everyone had been shooting fireworks and had not been bothered by the police, but because Shorty's explosion was so awesome, apparently the police thought there was a accident or some type to tragedy.

Never in my life have I seen a more awesome and unusual scene pertaining to fireworks.

Rick, John and I sure did have a great time with Shorty, but the time came when we had to say good bye.

I never did know the mans name, but when we met him he was called Shorty. When he left us he was called the Pyrotech Kid. The Pyrotech Kid was from Georgia and was now in his truck and heading home. I wish him the best of luck and I sure hope the Pyrotech Kid don't have a blow out, because he has way too many explosions already. Long live my good buddy, the Pyrotech Kid.

TINY LUND SAVED MY LIFE

Tiny Lund is a giant of a man. I don't know his exact statistics, but I can give you some approximate information on his size. Tiny was about 6' 5" tall and weighed about 300 pounds. He was not only big, but he was also rough, tough and strong. He was also known to be one heck of a fighter when he needed to do so. First of all, please let me tell you the better side of Tiny. Tiny was a very good driver and almost everyone love him. He was so much respected by everyone including his peers. He was always there when anyone in trouble needed his help. He friends loved him like a brother and Tiny seemed to love everyone.

Tiny's love for his fellow drivers was proven at Daytona Speedway in 1963 when he saved the life of Marvin Panch. Marvin Panch was driving the #21 Ford for the Wood Brothers during a practice session leading up to the Daytona 500. Panch wreck his car it it burst into a huge ball of fire. When Tiny saw the car in flames, he knew that Panch would have a hard time getting out of the car. Tiny ran to the car, ran into the flames, grabbed Panch by the arms and pulled him out of the burning inferno. Panch was burned very seriously, but it was not life threatening. However, Panch was burned so bad that he would not be able to drive in the upcoming Daytona 500.

Panch told the Wood Brothers, that if had not been for Tiny, he would have died in that ball of flame. Panch recommended to the Wood Brothers, for them to let Tiny drive his back up car in the Daytona 500. The Wood Brothers agreed with Panch and was more than happy to give Tiny the ride.

Tiny Lund had been driving for a long time, before this event happened, but he had never had a top quality car to prove his ability as a driver.

This ending is almost like a fairy tale, but it is true. Tiny Lund went on to win the Daytona 500. No driver has ever deserved a win more than Tiny Lund did on that day. Maybe he reaped what he sowed and his seed must have been very good. YeeHawee to a great driver, Tiny Lund.

PISTOL PACKIN' MOMMA, ELIZABETH

The story that I am beginning to tell is one that I sure would have liked to witnessed. However, I was not present that day to see this very interesting event.

Tiny Lund is a giant of a man. I don't know his exact statistics, but I can give you some approximate information on his size. Tiny was about 6' 5" tall and weighed about 300 pounds. He was not only big, but he was also rough, tough and strong. He was also known to be one heck of a fighter when he needed to do so. First of all, please let me tell you the better side of Tiny. Tiny was a very good driver and almost everyone loved him. He was very much respected by everyone including his peers. He was always there when anyone in trouble needed his help. He friends loved him like a brother and Tiny seemed to love everyone. Back in the early days of racing when Lee petty was one of the best hot dogs in racing. He was a tough driver and sure did know how to handle that # 42 to get it to the checker flag. He also knew how to be rough, reckless and sometimes practiced over doing it a little bit. This is the story about the day that Lee more than met his match when he and Tiny

Lund got into a argument, that eventually turned into a fight. Richard and Maurice, who were Lee's two sons were teenagers at the time and they were in the pits sitting with their mother ELIZABETH.

During the race there was a lot of beating, banking, slamming and bumping taking place between Lee Petty and Tiny Lund. This process keep going for several laps until it finally ended with a bunch of wrecked cars.

Finally, Lee and Tiny came face to face and the fight was on. Lee was beating on Tiny and Tiny was picking Lee up and throwing him down on the ground. There was no way that Lee was going to whip Tiny in a fair fight. The fight kept going, but it seemed that Tiny didn't want to really hurt Lee, but he was more interested in being on the defense to protect himself.

Richard was watching and could see that his daddy needed help. Richard ran up to Tiny and Tiny did him exactly like he had done his daddy by picking him up in the air and throwing him down on the ground. Well, I guess Maurice thought they needed him, so into the fight he went. There was Lee, Richard and Maurice fighting Tiny Lund and Tiny was still throwing then any way but loose.

All of a sudden, Lee's wife ELIZABETH thought she would get a piece of Tiny, so into the fight she went. Elizabeth had a big black pocketbook with two handles on it. She was hanging on to those handles as tight as she could and she was banging Tiny in the head with the pocketbook. Tiny was not trying to hurt her, but she sure was trying to hurt him. She beat on Tiny so much that he forgot about Lee, Richard and Maurice and just tried to run away from Elizabeth before she beat him to death with a pocketbook that had something heavy inside.

OH, you may ask. What was inside her pocketbook. According to security guards at the speedway. When they opened the pocketbook they found a Smith and Wesson .38 special Pistol.

Maybe we can learn something from this story. If we ever get into a fight with a man and see a Pistol Packin' Momma running toward us with a pocketbook, then we had better start hauling ass. YeeHawee to ELIZABETH and thanks to Tiny for the memories.

CREW CHIEF, DALE INMAN

I am sure that all of you older racing fans know who I am talking about when I say he won more races than any other crew chief in history. Yes, that is Dale Inman. Dale Inman is Richard Petty's first cousin and was the crew chief for Richard during most of his life. Richard, Dale and Maurice were all like brothers and played together when they were children. When you see one, you would see the other two. When Lee Petty was the big dog in racing, Richard, Dale and Maurice use to help work on Lee's car after school and on weekends. They also went to most races with Lee. They were just teenagers at the time. As time went by Richard wanted to drive a race car. Richard's dream came true and he started driving in the late 50's. (I will tell the story about how Richard got started driving in another chapter of this book). When Richard started driving, Maurice and Dale was a part of his crew and helped him work on the car, get it to the race track and was part of his crew during the race. At that time Maurice and Dale were a little too young to be a crew chief and that duty was performed by some older racing friends of the Petty's.

After racing for a few years, Richard and his crew finally found victory lane at the Charlotte Fairgrounds in 1960. That was the first of 200 wins that would follow.

By this time Maurice and Dale had become two of the top mechanics on the racing circuit. They were so good that Maurice started building engines for the Petty organization and was crew chief at the races. After a few years Petty Enterprises determined that Maurice needed more time in the engine room to build engines for Richard. That was the day that Dale Inman became the crew chief for Richard. Little did Dale know at the time that he would end up winning more races than any other crew chief in history.

From this time forward. Dale was the crew chief for every one of Richard's wins up to and including the 1981 Daytona 500. However, there were some problems in the PE organization the caused Dale Inman to be unhappy and he wanted to leave PE. After Richard won the 1981 Daytona 500, Dale was being interviewed by Ned Jarrett on CBS TV when he let it be know that he was leaving the Petty organization.

Dale Inman did leave with tears in his eyes, when he joined the Billy Hagen team with driver Terry Labonte. While with Billy Hagen, Dale and Terry just seemed to click and the chemistry was perfect between the two. They were a great team together. Dale with his great experience, to guide a young and talented, hard charging Terry Labonte. Terry went on to win the Winston Cup Championship under the great leadership of Dale Inman. YeeHawee is in order for Terry Labonte and Dale Inman.

TERRY LABONTE AND HIS CLASSMATES.

Several years ago when Terry Labonte was driving for Junior Johnson in the Budweiser car, my brother Rick and I were at Talladega to see the race. We got to our campground on Thursday, got our campsite set up and was just relaxing and enjoying being at Talladega. About 2 hours later a truck with a Texas license plate pulled in and decided to camp real close to us. There were two men in the truck. When they got out they came over to us and introduced themselves to us. It has been so long ago that I have forgotten what their names were.

However, the names are not important but what we leaned about them is the main point. The two men started unloading the truck pitching their tent. Rick and I always try to help other campers put up their tents so that it would be easier for them and also it is a good way to make friends and get acquainted.

After we got the tent pitched, we all sat down and started talking. One man told us they were from Chorpis Christy, TX. Then the second man said we both graduated from high school with Terry Labonte. That sounded like a very interesting story, but here is what really raised our eyebrows. They said that Terry was coming to their campsite tomorrow after qualifying for the race. I guess you are already thinking the same thing that I was thinking at the time. Sure, this was just a bunch of big bull that was being fed to us. Rick and I just could not believe that these guys knew Terry well enough that he would find time in his busy schedule, to come an visit them at the campground. However, we will just have to wait and see.

The next day we went to qualifying and when we saw Terry come on the track, you can bet the first thing that came to our mind were the two Texas men we had met at our camp. When qualifying was over we went to the campsite. When we got there our two new friends were already there and were sitting around drinking Budweiser. We asked them if they enjoyed the qualifying and we started talking about racing in general. After about 3 hours we looked up and could see a red and white

Budweiser van pulling into the campground and driving toward. One of the men jumped up and said, hey guys there comes Terry. I could very well see that it really was Terry. It was hard for me to believe, but the men had been telling the truth all of the time and we had been laughing inside because we never believed them. When Terry got out of the van he came up to both men and they begin to hug and rough house with each other. It was no doubt now that the friendship between Terry and them was genuine.

Rick and I started talking to Terry and we sure was enjoying it. Terry was a very nice person and he was so friendly to all of us. Terry passed out some decals, Bud huggies and some pictures to all of us. I guess I have learned my lesson by realizing that just a ordinary person like our two friends could have graduated with the president of the United States, because at that time the president would have been ordinary. YeeHawee to my two Texas friends.

NO. 1 BOUNCER ON THE TOOTIE BUS

My friend Tootie, owned a bus touring company and would take me and about 40 other friends on chartered racing tours. Sometimes the partying got out of hand and he had to hire a big giant of a bouncer to maintain control. Well, that didn't work out and he hired another man as big as BIG SHOW to calm things down. The problem did not get better and he had decided to discontinue the trips.

Now, I love to go to the races on his bus and I sure didn't want it discontinued. I told TOOTIE to make me the bouncer and I would try to help him solve the problem. Lord knows, that I could never take on that bunch with my physical strength because I am 5' 6" and only weigh 135 pounds. However, I did realize that those big giants was what caused the problem in the first place. After having a few laughs I was declared the Bouncer.

When it was time to go to Atlanta, I boarded the bus and TOOTIE introduced me as the bouncer. Everyone started laugh, joking and having fun while each picked me up over their heads and started passing me back and forth between them. Well, believe it or not we have had more fun than a bunch of monkeys and never did have any more problems on the bus.

This No. 1 Bouncer award was given to me at my 2000 Daytona 500 Party.

BOB AND THE LITTLE RED ROOSTER

One of my best racing friend is named Bob. Bob and I have had some of the greatest racing trips together that one could ever imagine. Lord only know how many times we went to the races together. Anytime we were together, we had a great time even it was filled by adversities and bad luck. It just seem that nothing could interfere with our happiness when we went to the races together.

In 1974, Bob, several other friends and I went to North Wilkesboro to the Wilkes 400. At that time I was a big Richard Petty fan and Bob was a big time, dyed in the wool, Cale Yarborough fan. We were at the track several hours before the race started and we were enjoying watching the driver, crew and everyone that was in the pit area. All of a sudden I noticed Bob watching so closely toward Cale's pit area. All of a sudden, Bob punched me and told me to look at Cale who was standing up on pit wall. Cale is a very short person and is only 5' 5" tall. Since Cale was standing so high on the wall Bob said it reminded him of a big Red Rooster. I thought that was so funny to hear him describe the scene.

From that day forward, my friend Bob was given a nickname and I started calling him ROOSTER. It didn't take long until all of Bob's friends were calling him the same. This little story became so popular that everyone seemed to know that the was the genuine rooster.

Several month later, Bob, about 5 friends and I were traveling on a plane to Daytons. All of a sudden I was Bob start shuffling through his little flight bad. He got something out of the bag and at that time I didn't know what the item was. According to him, he had something that was going to crack us up and he was just waiting for the right opportunity to pull it on us. Sure enough that opportunity came for him.

I had passed the word to our friends that we would all yell Red Rooster at the same. That was just what Bob was waiting for so that he could spring the surprise on us. Bob stood up, reached under his seat and pulled out the ugliest puppet rooster that you had ever seen in your life. We were all laughing so much that it started drawing attention from the other passengers on the plane. Sure enough everyone knew the joke about Bob and the Red Rooster.

Last, but not least here is the ultimate climax to the Red Rooster story. About a year our same old group went to Charlotte to a race. We were staying in the Holiday Inn on Tryon Street. We were all getting hungry and decided that we would go to some nice restaurant and have dinner. We all started talking and trying to decide where we would go to eat dinner. We had been kidding Bob as usual about the Red Rooster and that was sticking very strongly in the mind of Bob. Bob finally, stood up and mistakenly said, Let's go eat at the Red Rooster. Without telling you, I am sure that you know he intended to say Red Lobster. Lordy, Lord when Bob said that, we all liked to laugh ourselves to death.

Those great times have gone and I am still enjoying the races with my other friends, but God only knows how much I miss The Red Rooster being with us. Bob's health is not very good and he is not able to go to the races anymore.

He is such a special and dear friend, that I will love and remember for the rest of my life. YeeHawee and cock-a-doodle to my friend Bob, The Red Rooster.

HERB NAB, Can you fix a flat?

In my opinion Herb Nab was one of the best mechanic and crew chiefs in the history of Nascar. I particularly liked Herb when he was with Junior Johnson and was crew chief for driver Cale Yarborough. Cale and Herb sure had the right combination of chemistry between them. The respect for each other was awesome and one that was so closely related that Cale and Herb almost were thinking the same thing at the same time.

Herb was crew chief, but at the same time he was a tire changer during the pit stops. There was one thing that he did so much differently from the other teams. He would put the lug nuts in his mouth. At that time lug nuts were not glued on the wheel like they are today. The tire changer had to carry the lug wrench and the lug nuts in his hand. That is, everyone but Herb. Herb would put the lug nuts in his mouth. He would use the lug wrench to remove the lugs, then he would move the wrench to his mouth and use his tongue to push out one of the lugs nuts into the socket. Then back to his mouth to get each of the lugs when needed. Herb had worked this process down to a fine art and it was saving his lots of time during the crucial pit stops. Other crew members tried to copy the technique from Herb, but could never do it well enough to save them time.

I can remember a story that Herb Nab told which was about him driving back to his home from Charlotte Motor Speedway. Herb and some of his friends were driving home from the race track and noticed a elderly lady standing beside a Cadillac that was parked on the shoulder. Herb could see even before he got to the car that the lady had a flat. Being the good natured and helping person he is, he pulled off the road and pulled in behind the Cadillac. The elderly lady had no idea who Herb was and didn't know if he was a mechanic or dishwasher. When the elderly lady saw Herb, she said, Do you know how to fix a flat? If only she had known who she was talking to. According to Herb, here is his story. He told the lady that he didn't know much about changing a tire, but he was willing to try. His friends with him were about to crack up when they saw that Herb was having fun with the lady. Herb had to unload her trunk, find the tire and lug wrench and then put it all back in for the lady. Herb at that time was use to making 25 second pit stops, but he said on that day it took him 30 minutes to change that tire for the lady. When Herb finished the lady give his ten dollars that Herb refused to take, but she kept insisting that he take the money. The lady got into her car to drive away and Herb told her to wait a minute because he need to put something back in the trunk that he had left out. The lady gave him her keys. Herb unlocked the trunk, put the ten dollars in a little box and shut the trunk. This turned out to be a good day for the old lady, but Herb is going to have to practice on those roadside pit stop. YeeHawee to one of Nascar finest. Herb Nab.

BOBBY and DONNIE ALLISON, Living on Peaches

I would imagine that most of you think Bobby and Donnie Allison were born in Hueytown, AL.

That has been where they have lived for most of their lives. However, that was not where they were born. Bobby and Donnie were both born in FL.

They started their racing career in FL on the short dirt tracks which was called the Bull Ring. It didn't take long until both of them were at the top of the short tracks in regards to most wins. It was commonplace for one of them to win a race almost every time they entered while driving in FL. They became famous in that area and quiet often made the headlines in the sport section of their local paper. Everyone was talking about this great pair of racing brothers and all of the other drivers were trying their best to compete and win against them. That just did not happen. Bobby and Donnie kept on winning one race after another, although they had a big problem and were going broke. You may wonder how they could be going broke and winning all of those races at the same time. The explanation for this is very simple if you look at the cost of operating a racing team vs the amount of money won from the purse. There was only one salvation left and that was to get a sponsor. Naturally, if you were someone who wanted to sponsor a race team you would be sure to pick the best driver and team. They found it very easy to get sponsors, but it was very hard to get the sponsor to pay the required money that would allow them to continue racing in FL. Each of them acquired a sponsor and raced as long as they could on that minimum amount of money. Something had to give. Even with a sponsor they were still going broke. Finally, that dark day appeared and they had no money left to maintain the car in order to keep racing. Bobby had heard that short track racing in AL was a big deal and the total purses for the race in AL was more than 3 times what they were in FL. The main reason for the big increase in purses in AL compared to FL was that the attendance was much greater and therefore, there sponsors would also pay more because they advertising dollars would get more publicity due to larger crowds.

Finally Bobby told Donnie that he thought they should get their cars ready and go to AL to race. Donnie agreed and they took what parts and pieces they had to build the two cars for AL. It just didn't work out because they did not have the much needed assets to field two cars.

They decided to concentrate on fielding a one car team with the best they had at their disposal. They worked about 2 weeks getting everything ready for AL. When they were ready to leave, they only had $12.00 to their name. Even though they were almost broke, they still headed out to AL. They left FL and headed to AL which was a very long and tiresome drive in the days before the interstates. They drove for several hours, while pulling the car on a trailer attached to their truck. They began to get hungry and stopped at a small restaurant to have a hamburger and soft drink. I don't remember the exact amount that Bobby said they had to pay for the small snack, but it was way too much for them to be able to afford. They got back in the truck and headed on to AL. On the way they saw a fruit stand and decided to stop. They saw some beautiful peaches in bushel baskets that were only priced $2.00 per bushel. Donnie told Bobby, that they was going to starve to death if they had to eat in a restaurant or store. They decided to buy a lot of peaches in hopes that it would keep them alive until they could win a race. They bought 4 bushel of peaches and headed on their way to a small race track somewhere near Birmingham.

When they went to enter the race, they had forgotten about having to pay a entrance fee to enter the race. They simply didn't have enough money to pay the fee. Bobby and Donnie talked the track owner into to letting them race and they would pay them from whatever they won from the purse.

As luck had it, the owner agreed.

When the race started Bobby was driving the car. He started somewhere in the middle of the pack. It was wild and woolly to see those car beating and banging on each other, but somehow Bobby managed to get to the front and become the leader. He lead several laps and finally he had a mechanical problem that took him out of the race. Even though his day was finished, he had turned a lot of heads and had impressed many important people with his driving ability.

Bobby and Donnie had just had their day and were now forced with, what will we do now.

Finally a man that owned a automobile dealership approached Bobby and told him they he would like to sponsor him for the upcoming races at several tracks in the area. Gee, how happy they made them. It was agreed that the new sponsorship would take place at the next race. Bobby and Donnie got permission from the track owner to leave their truck and car parked on the property owned by the race track. They had planned to sleep in the truck and eat lots of peaches for the coming week until they received the sponsorship money from the car dealer. It was peaches for breakfast, peaches for lunch and peaches for dinner. However, they did have enough to fill their stomachs and kill the hunger pain.

When it was time to race the following Friday night Bobby received the sponsorship money from the car dealer. He was also lucky and won the race. You may say this was the very beginning of a great racing career for both of the drivers. It didn't take long until they had enough money to field a second car for Donnie who also had a sponsor. Life was great for them and they collected many win, one right after the other. Things was going so well for them that they decided to make AL their new home. As time went by, they were later the beginning part of what was called the Alabama Gang, that consisted of Bobby, Donnie, Red Farmer, Neil Bonnett and later Davey Allison. I am sure you know the rest of that story.

In closing I would like to tell you what Donnie said about the peaches. He said, (in paraphrase) "Those peaches were so good that I ate the seeds, but they saved my life. I am so sick of peaches that I will never eat another one as long as I live". YeeHawee to Bobby, Donnie and their 4 bushels of peaches.

BOBBY ISAAC, I Heard a Voice

I am sure that almost all of you have heard about Bobby Isaac. For those of you that have not heard of him, then please let tell you what a great and exciting time you have missed.

Bobby Isaac was one of the all time greats in WC racing. He was most famous when he was driving the #71 K and K Insurance car that was crew chiefed by the legendary Harry Hyde. Bobby was a very quiet man, not very flamboyant and if anything he was a little shy. He was never big with words, but he sure could let his driving do the talking for him whenever he was in his car. I realize that statistics are sometimes boring and if you desire to know more about him, it is very easily accessed on the Internet. However, I have heard many stories in my past 46 years that you will not find. My story that I am beginning to tell about Bobby Isaac, is interesting and as a matter of fact it is weird. It will really cause you to sit up and listen then it will give you a opportunity to sit back and think about premonitions. When you read this, I would like for you to exercise you brain for a while, to decide if you believe in premonitions.

At Talladega a few years ago Bobby was driving in the race. He had been doing very well in the race and had led several laps and always remained in the top 5. About half way through the race, Harry Hyde noticed that Bobby had slowed somewhat from his speed which was clocked the lap before. Harry knew something was wrong and though there was some type of problem with the car. A few laps went by then the car started to pick up in speed again. He communicated by pit board with Bobby and asked what was happening. There was no answer from Bobby. At that time most communication was done with the pit board from the crew chief to the driver, even though they had a small time communication by using a radio that was no more dependable than a walkie talkie. When Harry got no response from Bobby, he could not understand what was happening, but he knew it was something out of the ordinary. Finally, Bobby radioed to Harry and said you had better get someone else to drive this car because I am coming in and will never drive it again. Harry was almost in shock and definitely could not understand what was happening or what would be taking place next. However, Dave Marcis had fallen out of the race due to mechanical problems and Harry had him standing by to replace Bobby. About 4 laps after Bobby said he was coming in, Bobby came down pit road. He stopped the car, unstrapped the belt and got out of the car with tears in his eyes. He looked awful and was white as if he had just seen a ghost. Maybe he did or maybe he didn't, but here is what Bobby said (paraphrase) to Harry. "I started hearing voices and having a vision of me getting killed. I could hear a voice say get out of the car. I was so scared that I could not drive any more."

Bobby got out of the car and was relieved by Dave Marcis. Bobby was so nervous that he was accompanied to the infield hospital by the rescue squad. He was given a sedative to calm him down and then was released.

Several month passed and Bobby never did decide to come back to his team and drive for them. The rest of the year the car was driven by Dave Marcis. What a break this was for Dave.

Everyone knew that Dave could be a winner if he had good equipment. This proved to be true for Dave. He went on and won several races in that car and became the full time driver for the K and K Insurance team. In the meantime, several months had gone by and Bobby decided that he would like to go back to the short tracks and enter some of the races. He did just that. He entered a race at Hickoy Speedway and qualified somewhere near the front and ran about one fourth of the race and died with a heart attack in the car. There you have it folks. Like I said at the beginning, this is a very wild and weird story, but it was true.

Has you brain started working yet?

NOTE: Sometime in the last few years, Harry Hyde also died with a heart attack. Do you think they may have a race team at the big speedway called Heaven? Here is a very deserving YeeHawee to Harry and Bobby.

CALE YARBOROUGH, FIX MY BICYCLE

Yarborough has always been a very dedicated family man. He is married to Betty Jo. They have several girls, but were never able to get a son that may follow in his daddy's footsteps. Cale loved his girls, but it just so happens that he don't get to spend as much time with them as he would like to due to his very busy and hectic schedule as a driver on the Nascar circuit. He was only trying to earn a good living for his family which he loved so much. However, he was spending way too much time on the racing circuit and not enough time at home with his family.

When Cale was driving for Junior Johnson, he finally realized that his schedule was way too busy and was taking him away from his girls during their very important growing up period. He was running the entire circuit and wanted to cut back of his time spent away from home. Junior had great sponsors, but Junior and his sponsors were demanding that Cale race the entire circuit. Cale didn't want to leave Junior, but he knew for sure that something had to be done in order for him to spend more time with Betty Jo and his girls.

One time after a race was over, Cale went home to be with his family. When he got there his daughter said she wanted him to fix her bicycle because it was broken. Cale told her he would fix it, but he did not manage to find the time that day. He left home again to drive his car for the next race. After the race was over he went home and his daughter mentioned the bicycle to him again. He told her the same thing that he had told her before, but he still didn't find time to fix the bicycle. Cale decided since he didn't have time to fix the bicycle that he would go out and buy her a new bicycle. That sounded like a good idea that would solve the problem for his daughter and would get him off of the hot seat. Cale went out a bought the new bicycle and gave it to his daughter. Did that solve the problem? No, it didn't work. Cale gave the new bicycle to his daughter, but she said she didn't want a new bicycle.

He asked her why she didn't want the new bicycle and she said, I wanted you to fix my old bicycle so I could have time to spend with you. That statement from his daughter sure cut his heart out and that was the moment that Cale decided he was going to do something with his racing career that would allow him to spend more time at home with his family. Cale went back to Junior Johnson and asked Junior if he would be interested in cutting his racing schedule and only running on the super speedways. Junior and Cale had a great relationship ship and were happy to be together as a team, but Junior was obligated to his sponsors and could not cut the amount of races that he would enter. It was mutually agreed between Cale and Junior that Cale would be able to leave and drive for another team that would have a schedule with fewer races. Cale contacted M. C. Anderson who owned a construction company. M. C. Anderson had just acquired the # 27 car that use to be owned by L. G. DeWitt. At one time Benny Parsons was the driver of that car. Cale and M. C. agreed on a contract and also agreed to only run the car on the super speedways. This made Cale very happy because he had been haunted by not spending time with his family.

The relationship between Cale and M. C. Was successful, but they never did become a super team. Later on Cale drove foe Harry Ranier in the #28 car that had Waddel Wilson as crew chief. Cale won several races in that car and the highlight of that relationship was that Cale won back to back Daytona 500 races in 1983 and 1984.

Cale was now beginning to see that old father time was slowly, but surely creeping up on him. He decided to leave the Harry Ranier organization and form a team of his own. Cale acquired a sponsorship from Hardee's for his new #29 car. He drove the car himself for a while and then hired other drives such as Dale Jarrett to be in the cockpit. Cale kept that team for a while and then he got a sponsorship from RCA. He changed the car to #98 and hired John Andretti to be the driver. Cale got his first Daytona win with that car as a car owner. John Andretti had won the Pepsi 400 which is the July race at Daytona.

From that time on it seem that everything was going down hill for Cale. He had lots of success, but the chemistry was not working with that team. Finally he decided to retire from the hectic world of Nascar racing and go home to be with his family and enjoy life. In my opinion there is a very good moral to this story. You can give your children everything that Mr. Green can buy, but the best and most precious thing you can give them is your time. I can just picture Cale at home working on his daughter's bicycle. YeeHawee to Cale and his daughter's bicycle.

MOONSHINE > THUNDER ROAD

Many of you know that several moonshine runners became famous race car drivers in the beginning of Nascar. They got lots of experience driving high powered cars loaded with moonshine while trying to out run the police and internal revenue service. Some of the moonshine runners were so great at knowing how to drive and leave the police behind, that owners of stock cars recognized them and were hiring them to drive their car on the race tacks. One of the most famous drivers was Junior Johnson from Wilks County, NC.

My new found friend, Michael Smith can tell the story so well and I am proud to share his writing with you.

NASCAR Has a Little Moonshine in its Past.

By Michael Smith

Let's face it; NASCAR racing is not like football, basketball or other so-called stick and ball sports. Historically, football is considered to be an offshoot of soccer and rugby, and basketball was invented to give bored college students something to do during the winter. Stock car racing, on the other hand, is the only sport that arguably grew out of a criminal pursuit. Young hot rodders hauling moonshine through the dry counties of the South needed fast cars to evade local and federal law enforcement officers.

Naturally, any time two youngsters with fast cars get together, the time will come when they need to see whose car is fastest. From humble one-on-one matches, the contests evolved into multi-car affairs run on makeshift tracks. Locals, attracted to the excitement of the contests gathered and it didn't take long for others to see the money making potential in charging admission to watch the contests. Thus, the sport of stock car racing was born, and shortly thereafter, the race promoter.

No doubt the greatest example of a moonshine runner turned race car driver is Junior Johnson, who at the age of 14 was racing cars full of white lightening whiskey through the hills of North Carolina. Johnson's obvious skill as a driver offered him entry into the arena of stock car racing, but the money from making and hauling moonshine was better than the potential winnings from stock car racing, and Johnson continued to ply his illicit trade until 1960 when mounting pressure from the authorities, including more than one arrest and bounties of $5000 to $10,000, caused him to switch to stock car racing full time. Looking back on those early years, when he burned the candle at both ends, working within and outside the law, Johnson recalls that many people probably thought of him as lazy, seeing him fast asleep on the hood of his race car at a local track. The truth is, Johnson admits, he was probably dead tired from running moonshine late into the previous night.

Junior Johnson would go on to be a successful Daytona 500 winning driver and team owner, responsible for grooming the early careers of young drivers like LeeRoy Yarbrough, Charlie Glotzbach, Bobby Allison, Cale Yarborough, Darrell Waltrip and Terry Labonte, to name just a few. In 1998, Johnson was named the greatest NASCAR driver of all time by Sports Illustrated magazine. Furthermore, Johnson is responsible for bringing the Winston name to NASCAR's premier racing series.

Without a sponsor heading into the early 1970s, Johnson contacted R.J .Reynolds tobacco. The government had recently banned tobacco companies from advertising on television and Johnson saw an opportunity to create name recognition for the tobacco giant while getting some sponsorship for his race team. R.J. Reynolds had other plans, however. When told how much sponsorship money Johnson required to run his team, the tobacco company representatives reportedly claimed to have much more money than that to spend. So, instead of landing himself a tobacco sponsorship, Johnson served as matchmaker to bring Winston in as the main sponsor of NASCAR's elite racing series.

So, today when you think of your sport of stock car racing, spare a thought for one of its early pioneers, a man who may have started out flirting with the wrong side of the law, but who eventually rose to occupy the ranks of NASCAR's greatest drivers.

I AM RALPH'S BOY

This story that I am about to write was one that I will never forget and one that I vividly remembered every time I saw him, read about him or even heard the name of Dale Earnhardt mentioned. However, as strong and important as that memory is to me, I can not remember the exact year it took place. I have lots of photos of that day, but they are not filed and it would take me hours to find them. Maybe this will suffice by saying it was approximately between 1975 and 1978.

This story took place at a little 1/4 mile asphalt track at Kingsport, TN. I went to Kingsport to watch the Nascar Sportsman Race, which would now be called the Busch Grand National race. Some of the Big Dog's racing at Kingsport were Jack Ingram, Harry Gant, Dave Marcis, Tommy Ellis, Sam Ard and others.

I arrived at the track about 4 hours before the race started, in order to visit the pit to watch, mingle and talk to the drivers before the race started. Back then if you had a ticket to the race you were allowed to go into the pits and stay there until one hour before the qualifying was due to start.

Naturally, I was like ever other fan and headed down to see the top stars, that I respected, honored and loved. I mingled and talked to the top dogs for about two hours and had decided to go back to the grandstand to claim my seat. As I started to leave, I saw a young man, all alone working on a race car. I started walking toward him because I was curious as to who he was. I had never seen him before. He was a tall, young and very lanky man. He didn't have a driver's uniform on, but he was wearing a set of rental work clothes like you would see the mechanics wear at a service station. When I got close to him, I could

70

see that his name was Dale, because of the little patch that had his name on it.

I started talking to him and told him that I had never met him and just walked over to get acquainted. He said, "My name is Dale, I AM RALPH'S BOY." Honest to goodness, that liked to floored me. I knew for sure that he was talking about Ralph Earnhardt. Gosh, believe me I knew so much about Ralph and his racing career and I was at the race when Ralph was declared the Nascar Sportsman Champion.

What a thrill it was to realize that I had just met Ralph Earnhardt's son. Dale, seemed so proud to let me know that Ralph was his daddy. He also was very friendly and seem glad that I stopped by to meet him. He said that Larry Uttsman's car had a problem during practice and Larry had to go to another car for the race. Larry had allowed Dale to use his problem car for the race if he could get it ready in time for the race. Dale said that he had about 5 other people helping him repair the car before I came up to meet him. He said that I am now trying to fine tune it and I will have it ready for qualifying. I told Dale that I was glad to meet him and that I appreciated him taking the time to talk with me. I went back to my seat to watched qualifying. When qualifying started, you can bet your boots that I was looking for Dale to see how well he would do. He was one of the early qualifiers and and I didn't have much of a benchmark to measure his speed by, because very few cars had qualified. You must remember that Dale was not in a top of the line car and qualified somewhere in the back. Jack Ingram won the pole. My favorite driver for this race was Harry Gant, but I just could never take my eyes off of Dale and was rooting for him to be the winner. However, this did not happen. He didn't do very well at all and finally left the race with mechanical problems that placed him near the back in the finishing order.

Like I said earlier, I think of this day very often and I can remember how proud he was to say he was Ralph's boy. This brings a new thought to my mind. Dale Jr. is now a superstar in the WC division and I am sure that he wishes he could drive as well as his daddy. It seems that there is quiet a difference in Dale and Dale Jr. because Dale Jr. don't seem to want to walk in the shadow or the footsteps of his daddy. I guess we can all understand why Dale Jr. is trying so hard to make a mark for himself, because he would have to fill a bigger shoe, than Dale Sr. would have to fill when he wore Ralph's shoes.

Since that day we have lost Dale Sr. who was one of the greatest drivers in Nascar history, but I am sure that everyone of you will never forget the Intimidator, Dale Earnhardt, Sr. I will forever remember him as RALPH'S BOY. A big Kentucky YeeHawee is in order for Ralph, Dale Jr and RALPH'S BOY.

DALE EARNHARDT TIRE TABLE

This article is dedicated to my son Omer Champion,ll (Champ) who made it possible for me to write this story. Champ is in the USAF and is training to become a F-16 Fighter Pilot. When Champ was a kid and lived with me, I took him to lots of Nascar races. He was brought up to work for everything he gets and was not taught to try and get something for nothing. It was sorta like Smith and Barney said, YOU EARN IT THE HARD WAY.

When he was about 16 years old, I told him that I would take him and his buddy Andy to the Talladega race. Champ started working to make enough money to be able to go. I had agreed to pay for his ticket, but he had to work for his spending money. He worked so hard for a long period of time and finally had earned about $90.00. We were all set and ready to go to Talladega.

When Champ, Andy and I got to Talladega we found all of our old friends that we had been camping with for years. Sometimes, we have as much fun in the campground as we do at the race.

We went to the race and after it was over, Champ and Andy said they wanted to go walking around and see what they could find, so I went back to the campground by myself. About two hours later I looked up and saw Champ and Andy coming toward the campground carrying something, but at that time I had no idea what it was because they were too far away from me to see. As they got closer I could see that it was a racing tire. Champ would carry it on his shoulder awhile, then rolling it some and sometimes he would throw it and retrieve it as he walked by. It was such a hot day and the race was held in July at that time. Champ was so tired when he got to me that he was totally exhausted.

Champ said, daddy, I bought you a Dale Earnhardt tire that he used in the race and I bought it from Good Year for $70.00 and it is identified by a coded number. My heart liked to broke as I thought about how much he paid for the tire out of his pocket from working so hard. Sure, yes, I did cry from happiness as the tears flowed down my cheek. What a honor and a token of love this was for me. I felt so loved, to know that he spent 7/9 of his money on me. Yep, I sure love that KID.

When we got home I told Champ that I was going to make a Dale Earnhardt table out of it. I built a hexagon shaped base for it which was made from solid oak. I had two pieces of glass cut in a 36"D circle. I set one piece of glass on the base, then set the tire on that glass and topped it off with the other piece of glass as the top. Inside the tire, I had lots of flashing lights, reflectors, checker flag background and several Dale Earnhardt souvenirs. On top I had every 1/64 scale car that Dale ever drove and 4 1/24 scale cars, including a Dale Earnhardt telephone car.

The Dale Earnhardt tire table, now sits proudly in my Talladega room and every time I go in there, I think of Champ and SMITH-BARNEY. Here is a big YEEHAWEE for you from the great state of Kentucky.

If you are online you can see the Dale Earnhardt Tire Table by using the link which is shown below:
http://community.webtv.net/yeeehawee/doc

MY NASCAR CHRISTMAS

Christmas is a wonderful time of the year and a time that we should remember Christ on his birthday. It is also about loving, sharing and caring for your family, friends; and as God told us LOVE your neighbor. We all sometimes, celebrate Wal Mart more that we do Christ, but for that reason, I have never been excited about getting Christmas gifts. I probably get less Christmas presents than anyone. I always go shopping and buy lots of gifts for my wife, family and friends to try and help them have a great Christmas, but I hardly ever get a Christmas gift.

Why don't I get a lot of gifts for Christmas? I have asked my family and friends to just show they love me, save their money and write me a personal letter for Christmas that show they love me.

That is the way it has been for me for years until this Christmas. My family and friends write me letters and every once in a while they will buy me something. I guess they do that to keep from feeling guilty. It has been years since Jo has bought me anything for Christmas, but this year she wanted me to have something special.

I went to the post office about 4 or 5 days before Christmas. When I got the mail, I did as usual by separating Jo's mail from mine. As I was sorting the mail I saw a envelop that had something to do with Nascar.

Assuming it was mine, without looking at the address, I opened it. When I saw what it was, I realized that I have received this same material many times in the past. I put it back in the envelop and noticed that it was addressed to Jo Champion. I put in with the rest of Jo's mail and never had any idea that it may be a Christmas gift for me, because Nascar companies always buy mailing address and send the material to all of them.

Now, you know me, I am too sorry to work anymore. When Jo came home from work, she looked through her mail. When she found the letter that I opened, I could see a puzzled look on her face. She kept staring at the letter and then staring at me. She finally said, "Did you see what was in the envelop"? I told her that I saw it, but I didn't read it because, I get it all the time through the mail. I honestly didn't know what it was and had no idea it was a Christmas gift for me. We started opening all of the gifts for Christmas. When it came my time, Jo reached me a decorated Christmas shopping bag (those pretty little bags that cost almost as much as the gift that we put in them) and when I looked inside there was the envelop that I had opened. I guess you have already guessed what is was, but it was a prepaid gift certificate of my choice to the RICHARD PETTY DRIVING SCHOOL. I was excited, but surprised to know what it was.

Well folks, I don't think Dale Jr or Ryan Newman will have anything to worry about, but this only man is going to drive an official WC stock car. The gift certificate left everything open for me. I have a choice to drive at any track of my choosing and I also can decide how extensive a ride I want to take.

You know me, Talladega would be my choice, but my family wants to be with me. My Daughter Melody and her family live in NC. My daughter Missy and her family lives near me here in KY. My son Champ and his wife live in Lexington KY. Choices, choices. All of my family will be able to go to Bristol or Charlotte, but only Champ and his wife Misty will be able to go to Talladega. Jo will go with me regardless of where I choose. That decision is still pending, but here is the latest update. As of now I will be going to Talladega on August 14th unless we decide otherwise. The school will consist of 4 hours of lecture, video, ride along and driving myself. I will be wearing a Richard Petty driving uniform and helmet. For my pleasure only, I will wear my Red Wing Richard Petty edition boots. STOMP, STOMP.

After the lecture and videos I will be able to ride along as a passenger with a professional driver. We will be driving at full speed which would be approaching the 190mph bracket. We will make 8 laps. Then it will be my time to drive. When I drive the car it will have a governor on it that will shut the engine off when driven above 165mph. Gshees!!! I will get to drive by myself for a total of 8 laps.

Well, there you have it folks. I don't know if Jo loves me or trying to kill me, but I will have a blast finding out. YEEHAWEE. Eat your heart out Dale Jr. Your buddy. Omer

J. D. STACEY, Car Owner and Coal Magnate

I hope that you have read the article written by our staff writer Mary Henry. She wrote a article entitled "Why Dale Earnhardt was The Master".

If you haven't read her article, I highly recommend that you read it. Mary did a very outstanding job telling her story. Now you may ask? What does that have to do with me and why did I mention J. D. Stacey? It was ironic, but she just happened to mention one of my friends and my Kentucky neighbor, J. D. Stacey. She mentioned that J. D. Stacey bought the Rod Osterland race team who's driver was Dale Earnhardt. When I read that, it caught my attention and I decided to tell my story about my association with J. D.

I live in the heart of eastern Kentucky coalfields. My dad, brother and I owned a consulting engineering firm in eastern Kentucky. At one time we had more than 100 clients, and one of them was J. D. Stacey. My dad had known J. D. for many years and they were very good friends. J. D. was one of the largest coal operators in eastern Kentucky.

The first time I met J. D. was sometime around 1975. J. D. was needing some engineering services and I had a appointment to meet him at Hazard, Ky. We met at a restaurant in downtown Hazard. It didn't take me long to realize the he was a very flamboyant person.

As the years went by, I was with J. D. on many occasions and got to know him very well. When the coal boom hit eastern Kentucky, it was more impressive than the California gold rush. The demand for coal skyrocketed and the price for a ton of coal increased by 8 times. Everyone in the coal industry could get wealthy if they use good judgment and were good managers. J. D. was one of those lucky one. It is hard to imagine, how much money could be made at that time. Many coal operators that I knew were making more than 50 million dollars per year.

I can't say and won't try to tell you how much money J. D. made, but I will say this. He became a very, very wealthy man.

Everyone in my area of Kentucky, knows that I am a very big Nascar racing fan. However, I didn't know that J.D. was a racing fan. He told me one day that he would like to sponsor one of those race cars in Nascar and I told him about how much I thought it would cost him. He just didn't seem to care how much it cost. He wanted his name on that car.

About a year later, J. D. formed a company that was called STACEY-PACK. After forming this company he purchased the race team for Rod Osterland and Dale Earnhardt came along as the driver. According to DE, J.D. Was very hard to work for and was too aggressive and demanding. Because of this Dale left the team. J. D. never missed a stroke when Dale left. As a matter of fact J. D. just became bigger and had his name on 4 more race cars. This gave him a chance to sport the STACEY-PACK brand on some cars and on others you would see 5-RACERS, which was referring to his 5 cars. J. D. was one cool cat and smoked special made cigars imported from Cuba at $10.00 each.

J. D's name was on the cars driven by Dale Earnhardt, Terry Labonte, Joe Ruttman, Tim Richmond, Dave Marcis and Ron Bouchard. He was on top of the world, but being on top of the world doesn't last forever, in less than two seasons he was gone. Before leaving, J. D. Stacey left his mark on Nascar and held the record for sponsoring more cars during one particular race than anyone else. YeeHawee to my neighbor J. D. Stacey.

If you have any questions or comments please email Omer Champion at pettychamp@webtv.net

NEWSPAPER BOY TURNS NASCAR FAN

If I live to me a hundred, this story will still play strongly on my mind. It has been so long since this story took place when I was 12 years old. Little did I know at that time, I would be writing Nascar Stories for racing sites, much less be writing a book called NASCAR YeeHawee Style.

I was born and grew up in a small town called Seco, Kentucky. The name Seco derived from the coal company in my hometown that employed all of the men in the community. The name of the coal company was SouthEast Coal Company.

I was taught at a very young age to work for everything I get and not expect others to give it to me free of charge. I must get what I want by doing like Smith-Barney said, Get it the old fashion way which is YOU EARN IT. I must have been the pet kid for South East Coal Company, because they always let me work for them in the evenings after school and on Saturday. I also worked for other people in the neighborhood. I gave you the above mentioned information, in order to let you know a little something about my background. Now, I will start telling you about how my working days as a kid, led me to become a Nascar fan. I was a newspaper boy and delivered two daily papers in my hometown. I delivered the Courier Journal in the morning and the Knoxville News Sentinel in the evening.

I was a big sports fan and I loved to read and hear about the Indy 500. I would also listen to the Indy race on the radio. At that time I didn't realize there was any other type of auto racing. One day when I received my papers to deliver, I was looking through the sports section as I always do before delivering my papers and I noticed an article that said, a new racing league had been organized called NASCAR. That article sure got my attention and I couldn't wait to maybe find some more information in the papers that will follow. As time went on there were some updates on Nascar, but very little was said about it.

About a year later, I saw a big ad in the paper advertising the upcoming race at Darlington. It also said that it would be carried on a few radio stations, but the stations mentioned were not the ones in my area. Gee, I was so excited and was very much hoping and looking forward to the possibility of hearing the Darlington race on the radio. The closest radio station to me was in Knoxville, TN. That was a station I could not receive in the mountains where I lived. However, It just so happened that I was shinning shoes at the barber shop when one of the men said, that I could pick up the Knoxville radio station if I would drive to the top of Pine Mountain which was at an elevation of 2500 feet higher that where I live. That make me so happy, but the problem was, I was now 13 years old and didn't have a drivers license.

Every day as I got my papers, I kept reading everything about the upcoming race a Darlington. The more I read the more I loved it and the more I loved it the more I realized that I may not get to hear it. ENTER MY DAD. I had talked so much about the race that my dad seemed to know everything about the transportation problem I was faced with. DAD TO THE RESCUE. My dad told me that he would make sure that I got to listen to the race, in one way or another. Dad had just bought a new 1950 Ford (cost $900.00 at that time) and it did have a good radio. Dad and his friend Bill, sure did come to my rescue in style. Dad and I rode in his new car and Bill followed behind us in his car. Where were we going? To me it was like going to heaven (almost). Yes, my friends we were headed to the top of Pine Mountain to let me listen the the Darlington race. When we got there dad tuned in the Knoxville station and then he left the car with me and rode back home (15 miles) with Bill. Before leaving me he said for me to be careful and don't do anything stupid and he would be back to take me home.

I will never forget how excited I was when the race started. I just knew that my day was going to be a awesome one. Especially, when the names of Ford, Chevy, Chrysler, Hudson and etc were mentioned. That was like the cars we were driving, unlike the Indy cars that are hand make.

When the race started, there were 77 cars in the race and they started three abreast just like the Indy cars did. Johnny Mantz won the race. When it was over, my dad and Bill came back to take me home. I was probably the happiest and most excited kid in the neighborhood.

When I got back home, I was so humble and I told my dad, that I loved him for making it possible for me to listen to the race. A little bitty tear let him down, as dad said, "I love you too". Hey, I haven't forgotten Bill either. I had been cutting kindling for a cook stove and selling it to Bill for 15 cents per bushel or 2 bushels for 25 cents.

The next morning I gave Bill two bushels of wood for being so nice to me. Thanks to my dad and Bill, they are both gone now, but I will love them in my heart forever. I think a big YEEHAWEE is in order for Bill, my dad and Darlington. I very good and highly remembered event that I will remember for the rest of my life.

POTLUCK YeeHawee Style

NASCAR FANTASY

Let's let our imagination run away with us for a little while and we will try to live in the fantasy world of WC racing. Man, how exciting it would be, to be able to own, form and composite together what we will call the Ultimate Race Team. Here is your chance to form, own and manage your Ultimate Race Team. For the sake of simplicity we will assume that all of the drivers, crew and other ingredients are in their prime. You choice will be between the years of 1948 to the present 2003.

Let's see how good you can be by answering the questions below to form your team:

CHOOSE YOUR:
1 Driver
2 Make of Car
3 Crew Chief
4 Engine Builder
5 Sponsor
6 General Manager
7 Promoter
8 Car Number
9 Extra Driver Teammate
10 First track you would like to run on.

Do you mind if we just ASSUME? Let's let the time period be 2003. If Jeff Gordon is valued at 10 million per year. The price for a top ticket at Daytona is $200. What would be the prices for the questions listed below in the year of 2023?

1 Top Driver
2 Top Crew Chief
3 Top Sponsor
4 Good ticket to Daytona
5 Price for beer at Daytona
6 Price for Hamburger at Daytona
7 Price for gasoline
8 Motel room during race week
9 Airline Ticket from Chicago to Daytona
10 What would be the price for a 2023 Cadillac?

WOULD YOU LIKE TO BE?

Have you ever tried to imagine how it would feel to be someone other than your self. Have you ever wished you could be Richard Petty for a day, or maybe be Bruton Smith who owns so many speedways? Here is a little test for you that will let your mind wonder into the world of Nascar racing.

1 Which one of the drivers would you want to be? Jeff Gordon, Tony Stewart, Ryan Newman, Kurt Bush, Kevin Harvick or Robby Gordon.
2 If you could own a race track which one would you choose?
3 If you could only go to one race each year, which race would it be?
4 Would you rather be Bill France, Jr., Bruton Smith or Roger Penske?
5 Had you rather have the best ticket to next years Daytona 500 with all expenses paid or $1,500.00 in cash?
6 Have you ever thought you would like to be a tv race announcer?
7 Who had you rather be Richard Childress, Rick Hendrick, Jack Roush or Robert Yates?

8 If pay for each job was the same. Would you like to be a Nascar Flagman or work at your present job?

9 For he/she. Would you like to me Miss Winston/Mr. America?

10 Have you ever dreamed or imagined that you would like to drive a top notch race car around Talladega at full speed without restrictor plates?

Do you think you could do it? Without the plates the speed would be about 220 mph in todays car? Does that scare you to think about it?

Good Luck and a big YeeHawee to you and I hope you get to live your dream.

TO TELL THE TRUTH

This section of my book is a very interesting section. Why is it so interesting? Because you never know what to expect and you may be reading some questions that everyone can see, but you answers will still be confidential and will remain only in your mind for you to ponder.

Now that this has been said, let see how honest you can be with yourself by answering the question which I have shown below. YeeHawee to you. Are you going to be honest? Only you will know:

1 When you go to the races are you a girl/boy watcher and spend as much time watching as you do looking at the cars, track and surroundings?

2 Do you drink at the races and sometimes drink so much that you pass out or at least staggering?

3 When you are sitting in the grandstand do you sometimes find a vacant seat and occupy it until someone comes to claim it?

4 Do you try to flirt with a good looking stranger?

4 When you meet new fans and have a conversation going, do you always tell the truth about everything you say to them, or tell a little lie because you may never see them again?

5 Have you ever gone through the exit of a bathroom in order to enter faster?

6 When you have been given back too much change from a purchase, do you give it back or keep it?

7 Have you ever met a person of the opposite sex at the track and did a little so called hugging and kissing?

8 Have you been a rude fan and cursed drivers and use profanity among the fans?

9 Have you ever wished that a certain driver would get killed?

10 Have you ever thrown a object on the track that could be hazardous to a driver?

11 Have you ever met a person of the opposite sex at a race and then went somewhere to have a intimate relation?

12 Have you ever been in a fight?

13 If you have been into a fight at the race, do you always say that it couldn't be helped and it was the other person fault?

14 Have you ever cut line at the concession stand or entrance gate?

15 When you use the restroom, do you mess it up because you don't care about the next person?

16 Have you every hidden and carried a item into the track that was forbidden?

17 Have you ever stolen something from a fan at the track because he/she wasn't look and you knew you would never be caught?

18 Have you and your friends ever turned over a port-a-potty?

19 Do you buy beads. put them around your neck and start looking for some woman to give them to for a favor?
20 Have you ever gone through the campground looking for something to steal.

NOTE: Like I said at the beginning, you are the only one that will ever know your answers. You and only you know the truth. It just so happens that not a few, but very many of the fans have participated in this type of behavior. Here is one more additional question. Are you going to go home and tell your wife/husband girlfriend/boyfriend the truth about everything you did when they were not with you?

Thanks. Here is a big YeeHawee for you.

IMPLANTING IDEAS IN YOUR BRAIN?

1 Would you like to be the owner of Nascar and be able to make all of the decisions and have all the rules made the way that you would like them to be?
2 I don't like the Lucky Dog rule that Nascar has implemented in order to hold your position during the caution. This give the first driver that is a lap down and chance to get a free ride around the pace car to get the lap back. I don't believe anyone should get something for nothing. I think you should earn it.
3 I bet if you had your choice you would like to a see all of the races run on Saturday night under the lights. This would be good as far as I am concerned and it would give us Sunday to drive back home.
4 What do you think about the Hotels and Motel rising their prices sky high when a WC race is in town? This is almost like robing a person when you look at it from a fan point of view. There are two side of everything, so lets look at it from the Motel and Hotel owners side. If you

were the owner, would you do the same thing and raise the prices. I am almost sure you would. All of the others hotels and motels in the area are doing the same thing. They will charge what the traffic will bear and as long as all the rooms are sold the prices will continue to go up.

5 I can remember when I first started going to the races I could buy a ticket for $10.00 and I was given a free souvenir program. What is the price of the cheapest ticket that you have ever bought? Also, what was the least money you paid for a souvenir program?

6 Did you ever go to Darlington in the 50's when they started the race with the cars three abreast. Sometime there were as many as 90 cars starting the race. The qualifying was for the purpose of getting the starting lineup, but every car that ran the time trials was allowed to race. No car was sent home.

7 I am sure that is is hard to imagine and I have never seen this, but it is true that there was a race track in NY that wooden board as the racing surface.

8 This would be a thrill for me and it happened before I was born. What a thrill it would have been to see Henry Ford race on the old beach course at Daytona. Now that would be a classic sight.

9 Have you ever gone or wanted to go to Mac's Famous Bar in Daytona Beach. It is located on South Atlantic Avenue. It is a small place that sells one pound roast beef sandwiches and beverages. While eating and drinking you can see the older Nascar races on a large movie screen. The movie projector that show the races is a 16mm projector.

10 Did you know that Nascar had its first organizational meet a the Streamline Hotel in Daytona Beach. That was the beginning of Nascar.

TRACK FACTS

Shown below are some very interesting fact about the Nascar tracks.

TALLADEGA SUPERSPEEDWAY

The fastest speedway on the Nascar circuit is Talladega. Talladega's record qualifying speed is 212 mph set by Bill Elliott in 1986. The name of the track is now called Talladega Super speedway. When it was first build and opened in 1969 is was names Alabama International Motor Speedway. In 1969 the drivers formed the Professional Drivers Association and elected Richard Petty as president. The race was boycotted by the WC drivers, but the race was still run using some WC drivers, Busch drivers and some drivers from he GT division. Richard Brickhouse won the first race a Talladega. Davey Allison lost his life at this place where he loved so much, but it was not in a car. Davey was flying his own helicopter to Talladega to help is friend Neil Bonnett test his car. When Davey, with passenger Red Farmer started to land, something unexpected happened and the helicopter suddenly turned up side down and crashed. Red Farmer was injured, but not serious. Davey lost his life. This speed way was built on a old Indian burial ground and some folks, believe it is haunted and a curse was placed on it by the Indian tribe. This is the place where Bobby Isaac had a vision and a voice told him that he was going to die if he didn't get out of the car.

One time some drunk fan stoled the pace car and drove it around the track for two lap before the police could stop him. This is also the place where Tiny Lund lost his life of the back stretch. Restrictor plates are now used at the speedway, but it was calculated by some racing engineers that if the restrictor plates were removed today car could qualify at 230mph.

DAYTONA INTERNATIONAL SPEEDWAY

Daytona International Speedway is called the world center of speed. The name was given to Daytona because it is host to WC, Bush, ARCA SCCA, NCT, Bud Shootout, Twin 125 qualifiers and also Motorcycles. When you consider all divisions of races at Daytona, Dale Earnhardt is the biggest winner, but he never won the Daytona 500 but one time in 1998. The speed record was set by Bill Elliott at 208mph. Richard Petty won the Daytona 500 7 times which is a record that may stand forever.

Daytona has been the super bowl of racing and many drivers say if you win he Daytona 500 that it alone make for a good year. The winners share is usually over a million dollars and when you add commercials, promotions, endorsements and sovereigns it would total more then 10 million dollars.

CHARLOTTE MOTOR SPEEDWAY

Charlotte Motor Speedway is in the center of the racing world, more than 80% of the teams are housed at Charlotte or the surrounding area. The speedway was built in 1960 by Curtis Turner and Associates, but was
facing bank bankruptcy and was taken over by Bruton Smith and Fred Wilson. The speedway's president is Humpy Wheeler and IMO he is the best track promoter in Nascar. It is the speedway where Fireball Roberts lost his life in a fiery crash with Junior Johnson and Ned Jarrett. It is the home of the world 600, now called the Coca Cola

600. It is the only 600 mile race on the circuit. It took Richard Petty almost as long to get his first win a Charlotte as it did for Dale Earnhardt to get his first win at the Daytona 500.

DARLINGTON RACEWAY

Darling Raceway is the home of the world famous Southern 500. Some drivers have said that they had rather win that race than the Daytona 500. The reason for this, was because of the history from the old track that was built in 1950. So many of the old time driver had driven in this very historical place knows as the Lady in Black and the Track too Tough to Tame. Hard times have now fallen on the old lady in black and she has lost he Labor Day weekend race that we all know as the Southern 500. That date has been awarded to California Speedway which is bigger and more modern. Money can destroy the track, but I will never be able to erase all of those old memories about Buck Baker, Tim Flock, Fireball Roberts, Curtis Turner, Herb Thomas, Little Joe Weatherly, Junior Johnson, Ned Jarrett and many more.

ATLANTA INTERNATIONAL RACEWAY

Atlanta is a very old track that was built in 1960. It is a 1 1/2 mile oval track with steep banks and very long turns. Each turn is 1/2 mile in length and each straight stretch is only a 1/4 mile. That is the way the track was at the beginning, but now it has be bought out by Bruton Smith and has bee refigured and flip flopped. The back stretch is now the front stretch and the front stretch has be redesigned to be in the shape of a D. They have added lights to the old track and it is now a show place and one of the most exciting tracks on the circuit.

NORTH WILKSBORO SPEEDWAY

North Wilksboro Speed is a 5/8 mile slightly banked oval and was the home for some of the greatest short track races in history. A few years ago Bruton Smith and Bob Bhare were trying to get a second race for the tracks that they owned respectively in Texas and New Hampshire. It is a very long story, but Smith and Bhare both ended up owning 50% each of the track. They only bought North Wilksboro Speedway just to get race dates for their other tracks. Smith and Bhare could not get along and neither of them would sell his interest to the other. Therefore, The track is still sitting idle and the weed have almost covered the once packed grandstands. Junior Johnson tried to buy the track from them, but was unable to get the two to agree. Junior is a native of Wilks County where the track is located and Junior only lives 5 miles from the track.

It has been rumored that the city of North Wilksboro is trying to condemn the speed in order to reactivate it to help the economy of Wilks County. When that track was closed the fans were very disappointed and we are still hoping to see the day come that the weeds will be cut and the gates open again.

BRISTOL MOTOR SPEEDWAY

Bristol Motor Speedway had it first race in 1961 and the race was won by Jack Smith. At that time the speedway would seat 20 thousand people, but all of the seats were not sold. I can remember going to that race and the ticket cost $8.00 and I was given a free souveneer program. The speedway was built by Larry Carrier and Carl Moore, Several years later it was sold to Gary Baker from Nashville, TN. The speedway began to prosper and finally Larry Carrier bought the speedway back from

Gary Baker. The Nascar boom was going on the the demand for tickets was greater the the number of seats they could build. In comes Bruton Smith and buys the speedway from Larry Carrier. When Burton started construction the seats just kept growing and grow. Pretty soon the seating capacity was almost 100 thousand seats. At that time Bruton could see that he could sell every seat that he could build. The construction boom was underway at Bristol in a big time way. After a few years Burton had build enough seats to top it out at 164,000 seats. Just Imagine that many people in such a small area as a 1/2 mile track. Some of the seats are up in the air so much that I have heard some fans call it the NOSE BLEED SECTION. For those of you who have never been to Bristol I encourage you to do so, but let me warn you tickets are really hard to get at Bristol. Of all the tracks on the Nascar circuit Bristol was voted the most popular and getting a ticket was like striking gold.

MARTINSVILLE SPEEDWAY

Martinsville Speedway belongs to the Clay Earls family and was one of the older tracks built back in the 50's. Even Bill France Sr. had a hand in the building and construction of that track. The nickname for the track is THE LITTLE HALF MILE TRACK THAT THINKS IT IS A SUPERSPEEDWAY. The track owners also boast about having the best hot dogs on the Nascar Circuit. Richard Petty won 15 times on this flat track that has curbs on the inside of the track. The track is also famous because it is customary for the winner of the race to get a huge grandfather clock. The track is almost in the back yard of the Wood Brothers from Stuart, VA. A passenger train is used to transport the fans to and from the little track.

A MEMORIAL TRIBUTE TO SUSIE

When you first view the beginning of this story, you probably wonder what it has to do with Nascar racing. Have any of you race fan every belonged to a Nascar Racing News Group? If you haven't then you sure have missed out on the opportunity to meet so many great racing friends.

I have been a member of 6 racing groups for the last 4 years and I have met hundreds of race fans that I can really call my very good online racing buddies. I have also met 43 of them in person at the race tracks that I attend each year. Never in my life have I ever met finer folks than I have met in those racing groups and met in person at the race tracks.

This little bit of background brings us the the main point of this story which is A MEMORIAL TRIBUTE TO SUSIE.

About 10 years ago Susie was involved in a very serious automobile accident that broke her neck and left her paralyzed and in a wheelchair for the rest of her life. Susie readily admitted that she was driving under the influence of alcohol and realized that it was wrong. She wanted to do something that may cause others to sit up a pay attention when it come to driving under the influence. She started her own web site and used it to reach out to the general public to discourage them from drinking while driving. I had so much respect and admiration for her when she came public and admitted
her wrong doings in order to help others.

When Susie started her web site, she was not a Nascar fan and knew very little about the sport. However, several of us hardcore racing fans invited Susie to join us in several racing groups. She was reluctant to join because she knew nothing about the sport. However, she joined our groups and everyone welcomed her with open arms and really dedicated themselves to trying to teach her the sport of Nascar racing. It sure didn't take us race fans very long to fall in love with Susie. She was so soft hearted, loving, caring, thoughtful and had a great sense of humor. She was in our group for about 4 years and everyone felt like she was their sister, brother, mother or daddy. In my case she felt like one of my daughters and she even called me her little daddy.

I have said so many times in the past that Nascar race fans are the greatest people on earth and due to the common bond they have between them, they become very good friends.

On Nov. 23, 2003 our precious Susie got her call from God and is now in Heaven looking down on us with her beautiful smile and she may be wearing her Terry Labonte hat. This story is dedicated to my special friend Susie, that everyone loved so much. Obituary for SUSIE.

TERESA SUE POSTLETHWAIT

Teresa Sue Postlethwait, 47, of 1606 Westfield Road, Jane Lew, died early Sunday morning, Nov. 23, 2003, at her residence, following an extended illness. She was born July 13, 1956, in Weston, daughter of the late Edgar and Marjorie (Sands) Barker. Her husband, Gerald Fay Postlethwait, whom she married Aug. 20, 1994, survives. Also surviving are two sons, Nicholas Todd Gould and his wife, Betty D., of Freemansburg, and Chad Cook of Jane Lew; one grandson, Zachary T. Gould of Freemansburg; three brothers, Bobby Weaver, Mike Weaver, and Jimbo Weaver; two sisters, Judy Weaver and Sharon Weaver; her father-in-law and mother-in-law, Ervin and Martha Postlethwait of Westfield; several nieces and nephews. Mrs. Postlethwait was employed by various glass cutting shops in Lewis County as a glass cutter with 16 years of service. She enjoyed watching NASCAR and collecting NASCAR collectibles, the Internet, and riding motorcycles. She was a member of Broad Run Baptist Church. A funeral service will be held at 11 a.m. Wednesday, Nov. 26, at Floyd Funeral Home. Interment will follow in Forest Lawn Memorial Gardens.

Hello Susie,

Guess what? I bet you are up there in heaven looking down on us with that wonderful smile of yours and wondering what in the world is that old crazy and stupid hillbilly getting ready to do. Well, if you will bear with me for a short while you will see how much all of your friends miss you. You sorta left us in a hurry and we didn't even get much of a chance to goodbye. I guess that is understandable when person has a first class ticket to Heaven, they may get in a hurry. When we heard the news that you were taking a lifetime vacation to heaven, it made us sad because we knew that we would all miss you so much. It made us happy to know that God choose you to be in His kingdom. The Lord works in mysterious ways, but the ways of God leads home. This old world that we live in is a wonderful place to be and I have found so much joy and happiness down here. I love it down here, but I hope I don't get to go to Heaven for a long time. However,if it is God's will to take me to visit you, then I will be willing to kiss this old world goodbye and let out my last big YEEHAWEE and say THANK YOU GOD.

Hey Susie,

I bet you wish I would quit babbling so much like Belinda and Stephanie and get to the main point of this post. OK, you win. I sometimes get carried away when I start to write about something that touches and comes from my heart.

When you left and went to heaven, I called Porky and talked to him for awhile. OH, BTW, the guy is crazy about you. He not only said it, but I could feel it in my heart through his voice. I also called almost all of your close friends and girl you should have heard some to the things they had to say about you. Sure it was all good.

What they said was so touching and it was so wonderful to know that you did not leave an enemy behind. Everyone loves you. Sometimes when a person goes to heaven, after a few days they are forgotten and life goes on. That sure isn't happening with you. Everyone down here is thinking about you every day. Life will go on with us, but I just wanted you to know that all of us will remember you forever and will always love our LITTLE SUSIE. Love, Omer

To Porky and all of SUSIE'S friends,

As I begin to write this memorial tribute to Susie, it reminds me of all the times that Susie and I would exchange emails. She was such a precious, loving and wonderful person with a heart of gold.

I realize that life for her was sometimes stressing and brought on depression. When she had these bad days, she would always send me a email telling me about her problems.

She was so very sensitive in regards to not wanting to hurt someone's feelings. She would also come down on her self sometimes and had a feeling of uselessness. Many times she would withdraw from our racing groups and say that no one was interested in her post. She was so particular about what she wanted to post and was afraid she would offend someone with her words.

Many times she would send me the post before she actually posted it in the group. She wanted me to see if I thought she would offend someone by posting it. Why was she this way? The answer is simple. She had a big and soft heart that didn't want to hurt anyone. She loved you and I very much and our friendships was one of the highlights of her life. I could see and feel the love that Susie had for everyone of us. That was the kind of person she was.

Many times, I have thanked God that Susie had Porky to love and care for her. Porky must me one heck of a nice guy and there is no doubt in my mind that he loved Susie with all of his heart. Porky, to you, I would like to say that I admire, respect and love you for being such a good husband to Susie. God knew she needed you and you were always there for her. Porky, thank you so much.

Susie told me several time that the most important and loved person in her life, other than her family was her caregiver, Carol. Susie loved Carol so much and she called me on the phone to let me talk with her best friend, Carol. To you Carol, I say thank you so much for taking care of Susie, a person that was loved so much by all of us race fans.

For the rest of my life, I will never forget the day that Susie and Porky bought me the HILLBILLY PUTTER. Such a simple gift, but how valuable, loving and important that was to me. I felt so loved that day and knew that she and Porky would always be my friends.

Another very important and happy day of my life, that pertains to Susie is the day that she called me and told me that she and Porky was coming to my home in April 2004 to spend the weekend with Jo and I. That made me so happy and I immediately started making plans for entertaining them. The highlight of that phone call was having the honor and pleasure to talk with Porky. Porky, was such and nice and soft hearted man that showed me he was happy to be my friend.

Sure there is a little hurt in my heart since Susie left us, but I know that she wants all of us to be happy. That is the choice I will make. I will be happy in Susie's name and every time I think of her I will smile and thank God for making a wonderful place in His Kingdom for her. I just have a feeling that Susie is looking down from heaven with a very big smile on her face and is saying I LOVE YOU to all of us down here.

I LOVE YOU. Omer

My RANDOM Thoughts, YeeHawee Style

I am probably the biggest HOW BAD DO YOU HAVE IT person in the world. I love Nascar so much and get so excited that I could write thousands of stories, but as I said, I will not do that.

Shown below you will find several Random Thoughts that are going through my old hillbilly mind. Since they are random, I will not be writing them like a story and in paragraphs as one normally would. You will not find them in groups that are all pertaining to each other, they will be coming out of my head as I type live. I realize this is sorta stupid, but I enjoy this type of thing and I hope it may interest you.

1 Richard Petty is my favorite driver of all times.
2 Dale Jr. is my favorite driver now.
3 I became a Dale Jr. fan because of his dad.
4 Fireball Roberts was my first favorite driver.
5 My favorite track is Talladega.
6 I had rather camp than stay in a motel.
7 My friends are so special to me.

8 Favorite race was was 1976 Daytona 500.

9 I will never forget seeing Bobby, Donnie and Cale fight at Daytona in 1979.

10 The races from yesteryear are better than today.

11 I think about Smokey Yunick all the time.

12 Does anyone remember Buddy Arrington?

13 #13 reminded me of Johnny Rutherford.

14 Drivers were superstitious about #13.

15 Marty Robbins drove #42.

16 Tiny Lund was called "Gentle Giant".

17 Curtis Turner was called POPS.

18 Charlie Glotzback got shot.

19 I liked Wendell Scott.

20 Wendell was # 34.

21 Best flagman was John Bruner. Jr.

22 John Bruner Sr. was Chief Steward.

23 They don't have a Chief Steward today.

24 I bet Brooke Gordon is happy.

25 Jeff Gordon should be.

26 Junior Johnson was a awesome driver.

27 Nascar stole my bicycle.

28 I love the first lap of a race.

29 Linda Vaughn was Miss Hurst.

30 She was called the Golden Shifter.

31 LeeRoy Yarborough was the first to win Winston Million in 1968, but it was not called the Winston Million at that time.

32 I am glad Bill Elliott was first to win it.

33 Hey, I just remember Harry Gant #33.

34 The women called him Handsome Harry.

35 It must be nice to be good looking.

36 Fred Lorenzen was called Golden Boy.

37 Did you know Richard Petty built a cabin.

38 Little Joe Weatherly killed at Riverside.

39 Worse wreck was Michael Waltrip at Bristol.

40 Pete Hamilton drove for PE.

41 He lost his sponsor because he could not fit in with the so called southerns boys.

42 Martinsville has the best hot dogs.

43 Talladega is the best place to camp.

44 Bristol is the best short track.

45 You may not like it, but Jack Roush is a genius.

45 Bruton Smith is a great business man.

46 I love paintings done by Jeanne Barnes.

47 Sam Bass is better, but not in tune.

48 Jeff Burton is not liked as much as Ward.

49 Jeb Burton will be a Nascar star someday.

50 The best driver today is Jeff Gordon.

51 Even though he hasn't won as many races.

52 I can't wait for the 2004 Daytona 500.

53 Those young guns will shoot 'em dead.

54 I remember when Lennie Pond drove #54.

55 Lake Speed said LORD BE PRAISSSED.

56 Curtis Turner was a millionaire.

57 I don't know if I should quit now.

58 I guess I should, but I love this.

59 Just read what you wish and quit.

60 I carried in coal and shined shoes to go to my first race at Darlington in 1958.

61 A new car then cost $2,000.00

62 I watched part of the construction at Talladega.

63 I have been inside Petty's homeplace.

64 I cried when Fireball was killed.

65 Cale nicknamed Darrell JAWS.

66 Cale owned #29.

67 Richard won 27 races in 1967.

68 Jeff Gordon will end up winning more races than 76.

69 Richard won 200. No one will win over 100.

70 Would you like to have all of the aluminum cans left after a race at Daytona?

71 J. T. Putney was a driver and pilot.

72 He flew me to a race one time.

73 Dave Marcis was a great driver.

74 He never had a full time ride very long.

75 Dave took over Bobby Isaacs car #71.

76 David Pearson said, Buckshot will be a good driver when he quits wrecking.

77 Buckshot's dad is part owner of Georgia Pacific.

78 Terminal Transport sponsored DW.

79 TT was once owned by Stevies' dad.

80 Bobby and Donnie lived 4 days on peaches.

81 I wish they would do away with plates.

82 Richard was in ambulance and gave the driver directions to take him to hospital.

83 Kevin Harvick needs to calm down to win more.

84 I can't help but like Bobby Hamilton, Jr.

85 Brian Vickers will be a superstar. Rick Hendrick sure knows how to pick them.

86 Right Jeff Gordon?

87 I loved the #3 Ray Fox owned car.

88 Buddy Baker drove #3 Dodge Charger.

89 Terry Labonte is the cleanest driver.

90 It was sad when DE wrecked him at Bristol.

91 I was a DE fan after Richard retired.

92 I also cried when DE left us.

93 I have a racing jacket that Richard gave me.

94 I feel sorry for A. J. Foyt. I wish him well.

95 Kurt Bush is not well liked.

96 Why does Matt Kenseth not get his credit.

97 RYR sure is on the downbeat.

98 Dale Inman was the greatest crew chief of all times with the most wins.

99 Almost everyone loves Bill Elliott.

100 I was going to stop here, but I think I will add one more for good luck.

101 I am only stopping due to respect for you. I have really enjoyed writing this articles for you and I really could go on and on and on and on like the Energizer Bunny, but I will call it quits.

Thank you for allowing me to be childish again by doing what I love most, which is writing about Nascar. Omer Champion

RICHARD PETTY IS THE KING

By: Mary Henry speedwaymedia.com

Richard Petty is known as The King of NASCAR, who can argue with that statement? Not Me. Richard Petty was 21 on July 2, of 1958. He once again approached His Father Lee about driving a racecar. Lee Petty gave Richard a 1957 Oldsmobile convertible he was no longer using.

Richard himself ran his first race. He survived and finished in the money in 6th for a pay day of $200. Richard went on to compete in 8 more races in 1958. He finished 36th in points. Lee, on the other hand, competing in all 51 races sponsored by NASCAR. He ended up winning his second Grand National Championship in the 1957 Oldsmobile. Back in those days the Winston Cup was called Grand National Championships. I received several emails this week, saying Richard Petty was also a 7 time Winston Cup Champion.

I in No WAY was taking anything thing away from King Richard. No one will ever Win 200 races and what 27 in a single season that Richard Petty did? 10 out of those 27 brought Him a Victory, and a trip to Victory lane. The Year was 1967.

When Winston joined NASCAR in 1972, the history books were rewritten. They all become Winston Cup Champions. That was the point I was making last week.

Richard Petty won WINSTON CUP CHAMPIONSHIPS in: 1972, 1974, 1975, 1979. The rest of Richard's championships were Grand National Championships. Dale Earnhardt won WINSTON CUP CHAMPIONSHIPS in: 1986, 1987, 1990, 1991, 1993, and 1994. All of His Championships came while Winston was the Official Sponsor of NASCAR. So My statement was a correct one. The point I was trying to make was that NASCAR is gonna rewrite the History books again. They will all now be known as Nextel Champions. Nextel was no where around when Championships were won. So yes, Richard Petty did win 7 Championships, just not all Winston ones.

Richard Petty actually was the first winner of a Winston Cup Championship in 1971. So now this leaves it wide open for any Driver to tie or break their records.

Right now Jeff Gordon has 4. He is the closest of any Driver. Use to ask all the time will these records be broken? Now What records? NASCAR needs to realize to some fans Winston was NASCAR, just like Daytona was Dale Earnhardt, and yes, Richard Petty had more wins there, but no matter who your Driver was you always watched for Dale Earnhardt. He was The Master at Daytona.

Richard Petty has most wins in Daytona 500, but Dale Earnhardt has most wins in Daytona over all. Remember the years of Petty Blue? 1968 He introduced us to the Road-Runner? Richard Petty has done so much for this Sport of NASCAR, and yes, He will always be The King to Me. A Special thanks also goes out to Junior Johnson, he was sponsored by Winston in 1970 Winston credits Junior with all their success in Cup Racing. The Petty's had the four generations. How can you write about The Petty and forget Adam. Adam is another driver that has been truly missed by so many fans.

The Petty Family to Me, has written so much of NASCAR's history. It was a joint Family effort to. Lee, Richard drivers while Maurice built the engines. Just like Bill and Ernie Elliott. All the names above are not new to NASCAR at all. But Fans just remember without them there would be no Nextel NASCAR Racing.

The Allison's, there are so many Families involved in this Sport. The Bodine's, Waltrip's, Petty's, Wallace's, Burton's, Yarborough's, Foyt's, Marlin's, Green's, Jarrett's, Pemberton's, Parrott's, Hamilton's, Elliott's, and so many more. History is a thing in our lives that is written daily. Hope to see you at the track.

Mary Henry speedwaymedia.com

GORDON SELLS FLORIDA HOME

Did you know that Jeff Gordon sold his home for $13.3 million. How would you like to own a home like that? Being a ordinary race fan I am sure that almost all of you could never begin to imagine owning a home which is that expensive. Since this is the POTLUCK section of this book, then I feel it is in order for me to ask a very stupid or at least a funny question?

If Jeff Gordon said he would give you that home free of charge with the restriction that you were never allowed to sell it to receive money: or Jeff will give you 1 million dollars in cash. Which one would you choose? I bet I can answer that question for the majority of you. You don't want the home just to live in, because is would never be comfortable for you and that is not the kind of lifestyle you want to live. I believe that the average race fan would take the 1 million dollars in cash. Omer

Gordon sells Fla. home for $13.3 million Proceeds go toward divorce settlement.   From staff and wire reports 11/13/2003 www.delawareonline.com : The News Journal ://www.delawareonline.com/newsjournal/sports/ 2003/11/13gordonsellsflah.html

BOCA RATON, Fla.
-- Jeff Gordon has agreed to sell his 23,000-square-foot Highland Beach mansion for $13.3 million, a real estate agent said. Gordon - winner of four NASCAR Winston Cup championships - listed the house just 48 hours before terms of the sale were agreed upon, said Robert Wyner, chairman of Barclays Group International in Palm Beach. The furnishings in the home sold for an additional $2 million. Proceeds from the sale will go toward a divorce settlement with Gordon's former wife, Brooke, who was awarded $15 million from the sale of two properties, according to court documents.

Brooke Gordon filed for divorce in March 2002 after seven years of marriage, citing marital discord. In early court filings, Gordon estimated his worth at about $48.8 million and his 2001 earnings at more than $18 million. Generally, Florida law requires assets amassed during a marriage to be split evenly, but Gordon contended he shouldn't have to split the couple's estate because he risked his life to collect it.

ARTICLES BY MY GRANDCHILDREN

As we all know, Nascar is a family sport and NASCAR YeeHawee Style is a family book that can be read and enjoyed by all members of the family including children. Children are so precious and it is amazing to see how those little minds function. Shown below you will find two articles written by two of my grandchildren. These stories were written entirely by them and they had no help what so ever from anyone else. In order to truly enjoy the thoughts that come directly from their minds, I have not edited or changed anything in their text. In other words, what you see is what you get.

"MY PAPAW IS CRAZY" Written by: Holly Baker (age 6) My papa has lots of Nascar stuff. he collects it. he goes to lots of races. He absolutely loves it. Tennessee and Alabama is what he likes best. If he don't go, he watches it on tv. He don't just talk about it, he is crazy about it. Maybe if he mist a race he would just cry his eyes out. When he has a busy day, maybe he would do that. Probably if he had to go to the bathroom he wood cry his eyes out. Papaw is funny. Keep this a secret about my papaw and he acts like a kid sometimes. Holly Baker

"ONE SUMMER DAY IN ALABAMA" Written by: Cody Baker (age 8) One summer day in Alabama there was going to be a race. All of the races would be there. When it was about time for the race my papaw arrived. One hour later the race begun. When they said ready, set, go all the racers took off. The one in the lead was Dale Earnhardt Jr. He was going 200 miles per hour. The one behind him was tighter than a bug to him. When he reached a curve he did 2 spins. Then he got started back. One hour later it was on 50 laps. Dale Jr. was still in the lead. This lap he was going 250 miles per hour. Then he got a flat tire. He had to stop to get his tire pumped up. A minute later he went back on the track. He was still in first place. One hour later is was the 100th lap. This time Dale

Jr was going 300 miles per hour. He was so much ahead that he passed all of the cars and passed the policeman with his light on. Then he came to the final laps. He was still in first place. Then he came to the finish line and won the race. Then he was awarded a 10 foot golden trophy. Plus he won one 100 million dollars. Then he was called the king of Nascar. He has never lost a race since he won that race. The End. Cody Baker

TRIVIA YeeHawee Style

1 What year was Nascar organized?
2 What was the name of the hotel where the first Nascar meeting was held?
3 Where was the hotel located?
4 Who was elected Nascar president?
5 The president of Nascar owned a service station that sold what brand of gasoline?
6 What was the name of the Nascar president's wife?
7 Before Daytona International Speedway was built, where did the car race at Daytona?
8 Who was Sir Malcom Campbell?
9 Who was Barney Oldfield?
10 Who won the first Daytona 500?

1 In what state was Jeff Gordon born?
2 What state does Rusty Wallace call home?
3 Name two 2003 drivers from Texas.
4 What state does Jack Roush call home?
5 Name two race drivers from the past or present that were graduate engineers.
6 In what state was Mark Martin born?
7 From the beginning to the present most drivers came from which state?
8 Name a driver from Spartanburg, SC.
9 What driver lived in Elmhurst, IL?
10 What state does Matt Kenseth call home?

1 Name 5 drivers that have won more than 70 races.
2 In 1970 what 2 very big races did Pete Hamilton win?
3 How many drivers have won over 100 races?
4 Who has won the most races at Daytona International Speedway, but won only 1 Daytona 500?
5 Who won 27 races in 1967?

6 What driver made the AMC Matador famous? 7 Name a driver that drove the Fabulous Hudson Hornet #92.

8 Name three drivers that drove for Smokey Yunick?

9 Who was the driver of the #3 car before Dale Earnhardt?

10 What driver won the first Winston Million?

These questions pertain to the year 2003.

1 Who drives the #10 car?

2 Who owns the #29 car?

3 Who is one of Jeff Gordon teammates?

4 Who officially owns the #17 car driven by Matt Kenseth?

5 Name two cars that Robert Yates owns.

6 What two drivers drive for Joe Gibbs?

7 Who did Jimmy Spencer punch in the eye?

8 What track is the most popular and almost impossible to get tickets for?

9 What track lost its Labor Day weekend race?

10 Who owns the #40 and 42 cars?

1 Name three drivers that drove the Tide Car.

2 Name five drivers that have driven for RCR.

3 Who sponsored the #17 when DW drove it?

4 Who drives A. J. Foyt's car in 2003?

5 What car owner is known as Cat in Hat?

6 Who owns Jimmy Spencer's car?

7 Where did Robby Loomis work before coming to Rick Hendrick?

8 Who does Kevin Hamlin work for?

9 Who will sponsor Nascar races in 2004?

10 Who is Don Naman?

1 Who is Tony Stewart's teammate?

2 Who is one of Jeff Burton's teammates?

3 Name two teammates for Terry Labonte.
4 What is Kurt Bush's younger brother's named?
5 What is the name of Terry Labonte's son?
6 Who is Matt Martin?
7 Who is Humpy Wheeler?
8 Who owns Darlington Raceway?
9 Where is the home of the Wood Brothers?
10 Where is the home for Richard Childress?

Who had the following nicknames?
1 Jaws
2 Gentle Giant
3 Pops
4 Chargin
5 Little Joe
6 Dumbo
7 Jocko Flocko
8 Humpy
9 Golden Boy
10 Buck

Who drives the same car # today (2003) that the older drivers listed below drove in their days? You only need to name one, but it could have multi answers.

1 Cale Yarborough
2 Fireball Roberts
3 Charlie Glotzbach
4 Buddy Baker
5 Bill Champion
6 Lee Petty
7 Marty Robbins
8 Cecil Gordon
9 John Sears
10 Darrell Waltrip

Name two different car owners for this same number.

Car # 2, 3, 4, 9, 11, 15, 20, 28, 42 and 71

1 Who was Bobby Hillin?
2 Who was a 1 time winner and had a brother that was a tv announcer?
3 Who was the only driver to win a race that was sponsored by Eastern Airlines?
4 What driver won a race for Junior Johnson and is home was in Canada?
5 Who said LOORDD BE PPRRAISED.
6 How many races did Wendell Scott win?
7 Who was driving the POP's COLA car and won a race at Talladega?
8 Who won a race in a research and development car crew chiefed by Gary Nelson?
9 What driver had two sons killed that were both race drivers?
10 Name three drivers that have the name Bobby.

MATCH THE DRIVER WITH THE CAR OWNER

Please select the letter that matches the numbers for these drivers and car owners.

1 Jeff Gordon
2 Tony Stewart
3 Bobby Labonte
4 Jimmy Spencer
5 Kevin Harvick
6 Dale Jarrett
7 Mark Martin
8 Brian Vickers
9 Jimmy Johnson

10 Ricky Rudd

A Wood Brothers
B Robert Yates
C Jack Roush
D Rick Hendrick
E Joe Gibbs
F Richard Childress
G Chip Ganasi

In order to spice this trivia up a little I have only used 7 letters, because some the drivers have the same owners.

Select the letter that matches the number for these race tracks.

1 2.66 miles
2 Lady in Black
3 The Rock
4 World Center of Speed
5 Recently Closed
6 It is not Watkins Glen
7 One Mile Concrete
8 Farthest Track South
9 World's Fastest Half Mile Track
10 The Little Half Mile that Thinks its a Super speedway.

A Bristol
B North Wilksboro
C Martinsville
D Talladega
E Rockingham
F Homestead
G Sonoma
H Dover

I Daytona
J Darlington

Please select the letter that matches the number for the drivers and their home state.
1 David Pearson
2 Jeremy Mayfield
3 Tony Stewart
4 Bobby Labonte
5 Sterling Marlin
6 Dale Jarrett
7 Jimmy Spencer
8 Cale Yarborough
9 Matt Kenseth
10 Johnny Benson

A Michigan
B South Carolina
C Kentucky
D Pennsylvania
E Indiana
F Tennessee
G Wisconsin
H Texas
I North Carolina

Note: Two of the drivers are from the same state.

1 What driver was called the Golden Boy?
2 Name the home town for Dave Marcis.
3 What was Fireball Robert's real name?
4 What driver was called POPS?
5 What is Buck Bakers real name?
6 Who was the Silver Fox?
7 What was the name of Tim Flock's monkey?

8 What is the name of Lee Petty's wife?
9 Who drove a Matador for Roger Penske?
10 What driver lost two sons in racing accidents?

WHO WERE THE FOLLOWING PEOPLE?

1 John Bruner
2 Harold Kinder
3 Bruton Smith
4 Humpy Wheeler
5 Dr. Jerry Punch
6 Barney Hall
7 Jeanne Barnes
8 Hal Marchman
9 Dale Inman
10 Louise Smith

1 Name the brother of Bobby and Donnie Allison?
2 Who is Richard Petty's brother?
3 Name one of Richard Petty's cousins.
4 Name of Terry Labonte's son.
5 Name Rusty Wallace's two brothers.
6 Who is Mark Martin's son?
7 Name the daughter of Bill Elliott.
8 What was the name of Junior Johnson's first wife?
9 Who is Brooke Gordon?
10 Name 3 people named Flock that were race drivers.
1 How many drivers have won 7 Nascar championships?
2 How many drivers have won 7 Daytona 500's?
3 What current (2003) driver has the most total WC wins?
4 Who is the second most winning driver in Nascar history?
5 Name 5 drivers that have only 1 total win.

6 Cale and Donnie wrecked on the last lap at Daytona in 1979 while on the first live broadcast by CBS. What was the results of that wreck?

7 Who won the first Daytona 500?

8 What and where was Richard Petty's last win?

9 Who was know as Miss Hurst the Golden Shifter?

10 What was the most significant happening for the first race at Talladega? Who won the race?

Where or how did the following drivers loose their life?

1 Tiny Lund
2 Little Joe Weatherly
3 Fireball Roberts
4 Adam Petty
5 J. D. McDuffy
6 Robby Moroso
7 Davey Allison
8 Kenny Irwin
9 Curtis Turner
10 Alan Kulwicki

WHO WAS THE CAR OWNER FOR THE DRIVERS AND CARS SHOWN BELOW?

1 David Pearson, #17 Ford Torino.
2 LeeRoy Yarborogh, #98 Mercury Cyclone
3 Buddy Baker, #3 Dodge Charger
4 Fireball Roberts, #22 Ford
5 Cale Yarborough, #21 Mercury Cyclone
6 Bobby Isaac, #71 Dodge Daytona
7 Charlie Glotzbach, #6 Dodge Daytona
8 Paul Goldsmith, #99 Dodge Daytona
9 Bobby Allison, #16 AMC Matador
10 Pete Hamilton, #40 Plymouth Superbird

TRIVIA, 3 LEVELS

Shown below you will find 3 levels of trivia. The 3 levels are Beginners, Intermediate and Nascar Professors. The beginners will be defined as those fans that have been a Nascar fan for less that one year. The Intermediate group will be defined as those fans that have been a Nascar fan for less than ten years. The Nascar Professors will be defined as those fans that have been a Nascar fan since the beginning in 1948. I think I am one of the Nascar Professors and I have acquired lots of knowledge, but believe me, I still don't know it all and I am still learning every day.

BEGINNERS

1 What is the car number of Matt Kenseth?
2 Who drives the # 6 car?
3 Who replaced Bill France Sr. as head man?
4 Who won the 2003 WC Championship?
5 Who won the 2003 Daytona 500?
6 Who won the most WC races in 2003?
7 Who owns Kevin Harvick's car?
8 Name a team that has at least 3 cars?
9 What car is sponsored by Dupont?
10 Who is Mike Helton?

INTERMEDIATE

1 What is the name of Rusty Wallace's wife?
2 Which driver has a son named Jeb?
3 Who drove the #3 car before Dale Earnhardt.
4 Who was accused of wrecking Dale Earnhardt that took his life?
5 When was Richard Petty's last race.

6 What year did Alan Kulwicki win the WC Championship.

7 Who was Alan Kulwicki's crew chief?

8 Who was the passenger in the helicopter with Davey Allison when he crashed at Talladega?

9 What is Buckshot Jone's real first name?

10 Name all 3 of the Green brothers.

NASCAR PROFESSORS

1 What was the Name of Tim and Fonty Flock's sister?

2 Who loaned Big Bill France the money to build Daytona International Speedway?

3 What was the name of the hotel where Nascar was formed?

4 What was the name of Lee Petty's brother?

5 Who was Cannonball Baker?

6 Who was first declared the winner of the Daytona 500 in 1959 and then later the win was given to Lee Petty?

7 The Hudson Hornet #92 was given a trademark name. What was that trademark name and what driver made it most famous?

8 When the first ever sanctioned Nascar race was held, how was the driver's door secured to keep it from coming open?

9 Who was the first driver to drive a car wearing Bermuda Shorts?

10 Union 76 is the official gasoline for Nascar in 2003 and that name will be changed in 2004. What was the name of the official gasoline company in the beginning of Nascar and what slogan was used to promote it?

If you have any questions or comments about this article, please contact Omer Champion at pettychamp@webtv.net

I am particularly interested in knowing how you NASCAR PROFESSORS did with this trivia, and I am willing to help you with the answers if you didn't know all of them. Thank you.

1 When Jeff Gordon won his first race in the Busch Series, what was his car number?

2 Who was the sponsor and who owned the car for question #1?

3 Who made this quote? (He taught me everything I know, but he didn't teach me everything that he knows?)

4 What very famous active WC driver won the 1979 ARCA race at Daytona?

5 Who won the Daytona 500 in 1979?

6 What was the name of Bobby and Donnie Allison's brother?

7 What color was the AMC Matador that raced in WC and was owned by Roger Penske?

8 Today the first race for a new WC season is always held at Daytona International Speedway. Where was the first race held before it was moved to Daytona?

9 Where did Bill Elliott win his first Race?

10 Bill Elliott has a son named Chase. What is his daughter's name?

11 Bill Elliott is now married to Cindy, but what was the name of his first wife?

12 What famous female country singer dated Geoff Bodine?

13 Who has won more races at Bristol than any other driver?

14 Bobby Hillin was a teammate to Bobby Allison. What what was the number of the car driven by Hillin and who was the sponsor for the car?

15 Donnie Allison and Cale Yarborough both wrecked on the last lap at the Daytona 500 in 1979. What was the car number for Donnie and for Cale?

16 What is Buddy Baker's real first name instead of Buddy?

17 Who was known as the "Silver Fox"?

18 Bill Elliott was known as a master of the super speedways, but had very little success on the short tracks. Where did he get his first short track win?

19 Who drove the #11 STP car for Petty Enterprises?

20 Wendell Scott was an African American driver. What was his car number?

NASCAR TRIVIA, About the Sponsors

1 Name 3 drivers that have driven the Tide Car.

2 Name 3 drivers that have driven the Valvoline Car.

3 How many drivers have driven a STP car? Here are your choices: 1, 2, 5 or more than 5.

4 What sponsor has been in NASCAR the longest amount of time? Winston, STP, Pure Oil Co. Union 76), Budweiser, Miller or Valvoline.

5 What was the name of the director of motorsports for STP? Here are some hints: He was the first man that decided to hire Richard Petty as the NASCAR driver for STP. He was also the man that kissed Mario Andretti when he won the Indy 500 for STP.

6 What famous NASCAR team was credited with being the most popular sponsor for PureOlator?

7 Name a driver that drove for Junior Johnson when the car was sponsored by Busch Beer.

8 What NASCAR team owner owns a huge portion of Hertz Rent A Car?

9 Who is the CEO of Speedway Motorsports Inc.?

10 What NASCAR owner was a professional football coach?

I hope you enjoyed this trivia. If you have any questions, comments or would like to know the answers, please email me at pettychamp@webtv.net

DALE EARNHARDT Pro and Con

Who Didn't See THAT One Coming? (from issue #19)

By Nate Dogg

Dale Earnhardt was NOT, I repeat NOT, an American hero. A real American hero is a firefighter or a volunteer at a soup kitchen. If Dale Earnhardt is indeed a champion, he is truly Champion Of The Dumb Asses.

I'm not saying it isn't sad that he's dead, I'm sure his son will think long and hard for about five minutes tops about the fragility of the human existence before he goes right back to driving cars as fast as possible until he runs until a wall and blows up, his insides splattering all over the bleachers just like Daddy.

"Dale was the Michael Jordan of our sport," explained Humpy Wheeler, president of Lowe's Motor Speedway near Charlotte. "To think he is not around anymore is incomprehensible. This is a terrible, terrible loss and, for me, it ranks right up there with the death of JFK." This sort of statement is not surprising, coming from a man who prefers to be called Humpy.

NASCAR isn't even a sport, for God sakes. Basketball and baseball are sports. Driving a car isn't a sport, more of a skill. I'm sure it takes coordination to make those turns and remember to pull over and get gas and all that. But can you name me one NASCAR driver who possesses a "athletic" body? I think not. These guys look like they were going to go man a schooner, light up some Winstons, and kick back with an 84-pack of Budweiser. If these guys are athletes, I hate to see what out of shape looks like.

Dale Earnhardt made Ty Cobb look like Shirley Temple. After Jeremy Mayfield beat him at Poconoco

Raceway last June, Dale greeted the other drivers by flicking them off. After seven near-death experiences from car crashes over the course of his career, Dale decided the most intelligent move would be to continue racing highly-flammable automobiles for a living. The always progressive-thinking Dale protested fiercely against restricting speeds, something that possibly could've saved his life. "If you're not a race driver, stay the hell home. Don't come here and grumble about going too fast. Get the hell out of the race car if you've got feathers on your legs or butt. Put a kerosene rag around your ankles so the ants won't climb up and eat that candy ass."

I guess getting your head smashed open is the ultimate macho act. The only thing worse than NASCAR is its fans. Put down a few hay bales, crank up the AC/DC, and thousands of dirty water coolers will appear out of nowhere toted by mullet-sporting white trash hillbillies, their hairspray queen love interests/cousins, and the illiterate offspring.

If they had a motto, it would be "Take it ALL off, sugar!" If they were a developing country, their main exports would be date rape, fruit pies, and NRA membership cards. Hang out at one of their tailgating parties for more than five minutes and you'll begin to wonder if Darwin's theory about the survival of the fittest even applies anymore.

Sadly, the canonizing of worthless celebrities does not end there. News stands sold millions of commemorative Princess Diana issues, a spoiled brat who thought having a cushy life wasn't easy and chose to get in a car with a drunk driver. What reason does she have for trying to kill herself, the tea is cold? The biscuits are stale? America came to a stand still watching body parts of JFK Jr. float to shore.

How many times did he fail his bar exam again? Sonny Bono, a sub-standard musician as it is, crashes into a tree because he doesn't know how to ski and people are writing Cher letters? Do you know any of these people? How have they enriched your life, really? Do you think they actually care about you? Most of us don't know the first names of our neighbors, but the whole world shuts down if Meg Ryan or some other idiot actor from California gets yet another divorce. For the love of God, start working on improving your own surrounding community instead of mourning over yet another has-been celebrating dying as a result of risks he/she chose to take.

Nate Dogg resides in Minneapolis and edits Ad Hominim, a quarterly 'zine that focuses mainly on humor, politics, music, and Abraham Lincoln.

THE BLACK HAT

Written by: My very good buddy Stan-Fan from Florida.

He would drive a pink race car. He would come from racing thoroughbred stock. If he didn't know how to drive a race car, he probably would have spent his life building houses, repairing the family cars, or installing tires at the local Sears.

Out of North Carolina small town roots, he would become the undisputed king of stock car racing, rise over its greatest driver, Richard Petty, and reign over its phenomenal rise from Southern grass roots, "good ol boy" style, to a national traveling billboard show which is today a marketing and advertising dream.

Along the way, he would make millions. Millions of dollars, friends, fans, fanatics, and raise the blood pressure of his fans, and adversaries, in the stands, and on the track, wherever he raced.

If there was a similar recognized name in sports, or celebrity marketing, he alone had the name recognition of the New York Yankees, with all the love and hate that legendary team generates in its sport.

Rock and Roll had The King in Elvis. NASCAR has The King, in Richard Petty. But he was the reigning Crown Prince or Duke. One knows all the records; all the wins; the whole statistical story is emblazoned in the minds of millions of racing fans throughout the United States. Little need to rehash it here. He was Dale Earnhardt, Sr., the man who relished racing under the black hat, and what he was to stock car racing was its undisputed star attraction and most intimidating driver in history. In fact, The Intimidator was a role that he gloried in, and played as easily as John Wayne could portray a cowboy in a movie. And he was just as big as The Duke. Whether you were one of his legion of fanatical fans, or equally a member of the legion who hated him on the racetrack, his stardom and talent couldn't be dismissed. He WAS NASCAR, winning championship's early in his career, and late in his career. Again, the statistics are meaningless. Millions of race fans at the track and watching on television, marveled at the grace, recklessness, agility, abandon and disregard for the consequences, as he raced his stock car into, and out of places no automobile ever belonged on a racetrack. Along the way, he left smoking wrecks of his contemporaries, ended the dominance of championship stars like Darryl Waltrip and Bill Elliott, and prevented stellar racers like Tim Richmond, Rusty Wallace, Mark Martin, and Ricky Rudd, from climbing to the heights and winning the Winston Cup Championship in his time.

As he came through the ranks to dominance, it was Dale Earnhardt against Richard Petty. Dale Earnhardt against Bobby Allison, Tim Richmond, Darryl Waltrip,

Bill Elliott, Ricky Rudd, Harry Gant, Terry Labonte, Rusty Wallace, et al. It was Dale Earnhardt, with that sly, Cheshire cat smile, AGAINST THE WORLD. And he loved it. And the fans loved it too. He was the most prolific stock car driver ever to climb into one of the lumbering, thundering NASCAR beasts. Run it he did, owning a racetrack named Daytona. Banging and plowing his way around tiny Richmond, Bristol, and Martinsville speedways. Roaring down the Daytona and Talladega straight-a-ways at breathtaking speeds. Cutting underneath his opponent after he had been passed, on the final turn in a patented move, few of his contemporaries could match. One can still see him cut underneath the leader at the 4th turn of ancient Darlington, and hit the stripe the winner.

He would race, wreck, be injured, even wrestle a road course like Watkins Glen with a broken rib, when his race car lost its power steering and bring it home to a top finish, and think nothing of it. Was expected, he was Dale Earnhardt, Sr. And he won at America's racing nirvana, Indianapolis Motor Speedway in a stock car.

One could not visit any NASCAR venue and not feel his presence. The very first stop would be the crowd around his souvenir track hauler. Upon entering the speedway, the very first look would be toward the front of the pits, where slumbering in the mid-morning sun, sat the most intimidating black automobile ever, the Number 3, Goodwrench Chevrolet. One could almost feel its power, strength, like a serpent waiting in prey, waiting for the toggle switch to be clicked and racing's premier driver, to set The Beast in motion. One could almost feel and see it thundering, snorting, flailing the concrete in your mind, as we waited in the stands for him to light the candle of The Beast. Light it he did.

Throughout a career that rewrote the NASCAR record books, he went from rookie, to reckless, to relentless, to regal in his passion for his sport. And along the way, he gave back to his sport, spare engines to low financed drivers, a hint here, a word there, from The Man, and a career was launched, like Ernie Irvan in the speedy Kodak ride. A side few understood about him, because he mostly kept it hidden behind that sly grin.

If you faced him as a competitor, catching him was iffy at best, and trying to outrun him, he would fill your mirror with that intimidating black Number 3 Chevrolet, until you slipped, got impatient, worried, frustrated, took a turn high or at slightly less speed, than, a quick bump and run, and in a flash, like Santa Claus sliding down a chimney, in a twinkle of the eye, he was past and headed for Victory Lane.

NASCAR has seen, and bred talent in racing. It has never seen anybody like Dale Earnhardt, Sr. redefine the sport, and leave the masses roaring in ecstasy or agony over his fortunes at the track. At any venue, half the spectators, and probably half the television audience was wearing his colors, and applauding his ability, and show while the other half was agonizing at his ability, frustrated at his success, and in some cases, in the stands, or the garage, downright blue blazes mad at his performance or antics on that given day.

As a new generation of driver's in young marquee idol Jeff Gordon, and the talented Bobby Labonte came along to challenge the master, their success would be measured not by their victories, but by how they competed and copied the racing style of Dale Earnhardt, Sr. And with success, the Earnhardt legions would turn against the likes of a splendid talent like Gordon, just like the Elliott, Waltrip, Wallace fans turned against The Man when he came through the ranks, busting bumpers, plowing fenders, burning rubber, and above all, winning, winning and winning.

If there is an appropriate end to the story of Dale Earnhardt, Sr.,and his racing career, it must be Daytona, always Daytona. On the day he finally won the Daytona 500, every member of every pit crew would line pit road, and stretch out an arm in congratulations, as the Intimidator slowly and finally rolled his Black Number 3 to Victory Lane. In the stands, those that loved him cried, those that hated him as a driver, stood and applauded - in respect and admiration - and cried too, he had earned it from his first day at the track. And in the end, it would be Daytona again, as, blocking the pack for his teammate Michael Waltrip and son, Dale Earnhardt, Junior (forever known now to his fans as simply Junior), they finished 1-2 in the Daytona 500, The Intimidator would perish in a senseless, unbelievable accident on the 4th and final turn.

If there ever was a racer nobody expected to die at the track, Dale Earnhardt, Sr. was the one. He was too good, too talented, damn, he was just too mean on the track, and had cheated death so long he just couldn't die in a race car.

During his racing career, the sea of black one saw in the stands at any racing venue belonged to HIS fans. Today, the sea of red one sees in the stands at the track belongs to his fans too, with their love and allegiance transferred to his son Dale Earnhardt, Junior.

In other sports it is easy to be moved to tears. The Babe Ruth, Lou Gehring farewell speeches in baseball. Hall Of Fame Inductee speeches in football. The grace and style and pride of an Olympic athlete as they win a gold medal, and stand on a podium crying and smiling, listening to our National Anthem. Racing is not like that. The speed and excitement, the roar of the crowd, the engines, the noise, the flying rubber, heart stopping wrecks and finishes, all are observed, but difficult for the fan to actually feel in his or her heart. It is too fast, furious, and over all too soon, leaving us breathless.

The closest racing came to an Epiphany would be the day that The Intimidator died at Daytona. Love him, or hate him, damn, we miss him.

Written By: PureWCup~Dave R. P.

Many of the younger NASCAR fans do not realize that Dale's career and popularity changed drastically over time. In his early years he was known as a dirty driver and not well liked. You could count on one thing from him. If he couldn't beat you he would wreck you. The early days on the dirt tracks in N. Carolina were that way for him. Things were tough in those days with no money and two unsuccessful marriages. A certain part of that image never left him and was the birth of his Intimidator name. A lot of his core fan base was made up of people from the wrong side of the tracks, tough guys and hardcore rednecks to be sure. Richard Childress and Teresa changed all that for him. No need to discuss that part of the story as you all know what success and big money brought him. A certain respectability but still a hint of that dark image. Many loved him and many hated him but we all missed him when he left us too soon. Racing has never been the same.

My opinion on that was a comparison to Black Bart and Snidely Whiplash. You always knew that they were out to do you in and only had to wait and see what they were up to. It was always, "Look out here comes Earnhardt, The Intimidator". A lot of the fun and excitement left with him. That threat was gone and most of us missed it because we always knew that you had to beat Dale to win... PureWCup~Dave R.P.

Written by: Kim H.

The whole reason I started watching Nascar Winston Cup Racing was because of Dale Earnhardt. About 17 years ago, I was at a local American Legion on a Sunday. There were only a few of us there, and we were all chatting amongst ourselves, but most were watching the race on TV. I asked a few questions about it, but that was about it. The next week there we all were again, only a few more people were there, all watching the race. I sat on a stool next to the TV, there was someone, I didn't know to my right, but he too was watching the race. I looked up at the screen, for lack of anything better to do, and I saw this black car, dodging and weaving, in and out of cars, and going very fast. I didn't take notice to the number or sponsor or anything, just how great this guy was driving. I think I sat there with my mouth open, and marveled at how well he maneuvered that black car. I remember saying under my breath "Damn, he's good!".

Well, it finally got the better of me, and I asked the guy sitting next to me, who drove that black car. He asked "the #3?". I said "yes". Then he looked at me, like I was from outer space. And how dare I not know WHO that was. I finally told him that I don't watch racing, but I was marveling at how well this guy steered his car in all that traffic, I said he was "awesome". This brought a grin to his face, because later in the conversation, I learned he was a Dale Earnhardt fan. He then told me that that was indeed the infamous Dale Earnhardt #3 Goodwrench car. He gave me a brief history on Dale, championships and such. I told him I had to agree with him that Dale was THE best driver out there. And from that moment on, I started watching racing, and of course my favorite driver was Dale Earnhardt.

It amazes still that, out of all the drivers I chose him. I just saw something in his driving that matched no other. He was truly gifted. I followed Dale and his racing for many years. His untimely death, really shook me. I'm still not over it. He gave me so much pleasure every Sunday. The void is still there. And no one will ever match Dales success and style. He truly was one of kind. And the best at what he did. I'm now a Dale Jr. fan. He doesn't drive like his Dad, but I see great things happening for him. He was third in points. this year (2003) and that says a lot about him as a driver. He's also a good person, one of the small town, good ole boys. Just like his dad was.

Thank You Dale Earnhardt for getting me interested in the best sport there is. And thank you, for all those years of watching a master at work. It truly was magical when you got behind the wheel of the #3 car!
Kim H.

Written by: Roy M.

I never liked Dale Earnhardt the first time I saw him, I didn't like him later and I didn't like him before he died. I don't like to see drivers get hurt or killed and I wish Dale was alive, but I am glad he is not racing anymore. He was the dirtiest driver I have ever seen. He should not have been allowed in the sport.

Written by: Tammy Bousher

The first race I went to was at the Winston at Charlotte Speedway. It was such a good race and I was really rooting for Bill Elliott, but when he had some kind of trouble the I like the Tide car driven by Darrell Waltrip. Darrell really had that car hooked up and no driver could have passed him.

I was at the race with my boyfriend and he told me Dale Earnhardt was moving in on Darrell and I had better look out for trouble. I noticed that Dale had tried to pass Darrell several times, but just couldn't do it because Darrell was good and real fast. Several laps went by and Dale still could not pass Darrell. It sure looked like Darrell was going to win the race. With about two laps to go, Dale tried to pass again, he could get just a little bit of his front bumper under him, but Darrell just motored on. Going into the second turn, Dale did the same thing again, but this time he deliberately turned right and sent the Tide car into the wall. Damn, I was mad. That made me hate DE. I don't hate his sole, but I sure hated the way he drove.

Ever since that day, I can't stand DE, and every time I saw him on the track I would stand up and Boo. I joined the club ABE which stood for Anyone But Earnhardt. I hated it when he was killed at Daytona, but I still never did like him.

One more thing I don't like is DE was jealous of Jeff Gordon. He could not stand it when Jeff would beat him. Everybody says DE has a lot of fans that love him and the rest hate him. I sure don't love him.

Written by: Charles Badford

I am 17 years old and I have been to 4 races and Dale is my number 1 man. He is the best driver in the world and he was better than Richard when Richard was a young man. When he was killed I cried a whole lot and I have watched the races on tv and it is no fun anymore. I like Dale Jr. now, he can't drive like his daddy, but I still like him. I don't like Jeff Gordon, He is too much like a girl. I also like Kevin Harvick.

By James

These are a few memories of mine of when I have met Dale.

#1. I had first met Dale in 1993 at a local track Lanier Motor Speedway it is near Gainsville,GA. He did an autograph session and me and a friend of mine were last in line. I had him sign a shirt I had bought off the souvenir truck that was at the track. It was a Black Intimidator VI tour 1993 shirt. I have never worn the shirt and it is now in a plastic bag inside my racing case. Dale was in his GM Goodwrench uniform and had on silver glasses. He looked like all of his pictures. Man I
wish now I had a camera. He later on did a race with a local driver Mike Love. It was a good race and Dale won. After he got his trophy it was off to the airport.

#2. I don't remember the year but it might have been 96 or 97. This was qualifying day. I had ARCA garage passes for the race in Atlanta and you had to walk down pit road to get to the ARCA garage. All of a sudden I see his black number 3 drive by and stop in front of me because of traffic waiting to get back onto the track. I still remember looking at him behind the wheel. He looked like Darth Vader or something sitting there. Anyway Dale won the pole that day and I had waited for him to come out and make his way to victory lane. Well here he comes and you had to walk real fast to keep up with him and I got behind him and handed him my program to sign. (it was all that i had on me). Years later whenever I go to the races I always enjoy seeing my favorite drivers make there way out of the pits to there cars and all the time even if I was far away I could always tell that Dale had just come out by watching the crowd swell around him.

#3. This is short but me and the Mrs. had met him at the World Congress Center in Atlanta for a car show he was appearing at. We were first in line. I knew what the line would be like and my wife had him sign a 1:24 scale car and I had him sign a Sam Bass Quick Silver Poster. He was very nice. After he signed it he told me to be careful because it looked like it was about to rain outside. I took his warning seriously and got some bags to cover the poster.

#4. I had seen Dale and Jr at the world of coke in Atlanta when the coke Japan cars were announced. Richard Childress was there and I had him sign my #3 hat and a Sam Bass poster. I did not attempt to get Dale's autograph because of the crowd but I got Jr's and had my picture made with him. He was cool. I got some real good pics of that day.

#5. I think this was Nov 98. Dale was appearing at a local car dealership. Hennesy GMC. Well I was 2nd in line. Dale flew in on a helicopter and landed at the mall next door. When he started to sign we were at the door and he came over and opened the door to let everyone in. Since we were 2nd I managed to slip behind the table and have the Mrs. get a pic of me with him. He winked at my wife and said that he had to get all the pretty ladies through here. He signed a Sam Bass poster of himself and Jr. I had already had Jr sign it at the world of coke. He had asked where I had Jr and Richard sign it. He then said that Jr was all over the place and I didn't have to go through the trouble at the world of coke (huh) anyway The picture is hanging in my living room along with the picture on Dale, Jr and me.

#6. The last time I saw Dale at an appearance he was at Sales Auto Mall in Dalton,GA. it was before a Talledega race. When we got there the line was already very big and we had heard that some fans were there 2 days earlier. He also flew in on a helicopter had him sign the picture my wife had taken of us. I think he recognized my wife because he had made a remark about the picture to her about him being better looking than me. LOL! These are just a few memories I have to share. Dale is the greatest driver I have ever seen. He was also a good role model to look up too. By reading about him and seeing him on TV talk, I can understand why Jr always set out to race for his dad. There was just something about him. Thanks for reading. James

Written by: Shirley Crawford

I sure would like to tell you perfectly how I feel about Dale Earnhardt. But, you can, you see because some children my read this book and you Mr. Champion, my not want to put it in your book if I said what really is on my mind. He was the most arrogant, hateful and most hated driver that has ever driven a car. Oh, I know he is a good driver but if I could drive as good as him, I would not be wrecking and almost killing the other driver by shoving them into the wall. He would run them down turn right and wreck them on purpose and then say That's Racing. Sure he say that's racing, but I call it That's Wrecking. Just ask a gentlemen, like Terry Labonte what he did to him at Bristol and the tried to rub it in and said, I just Rattled His Cage. I would be ashame to wreck someone like Terry. I am a Jeff Gordon fan and he could out drive Dale any day and did when Dale didn't wreck him. I will close and say he stinks like the world's biggest skunk.

Written by: Elizabeth Weaver

My dad has been a Dale Earnhardt fan since I could well at least try to learn to talk back in '87. I remember on Sunday afternoons watching the black #3 and shouting go Dale Winhardt since I couldn't for some unknown reason say Earnhardt at the time. When I was about 6 years old I met Dale Earnhardt. I was so star struck that I fell off the stage he was sitting on! He got up, made sure I was ok and gently helped me to my feet. I stopped watching racing until Dale Jr. came on the scene. (like every teen girl!) So now every Sunday I watch what my dad once seen in Dale Earnhardt show up in the eyes and ways of the new great-Dale Earnhardt Jr. Elizabeth Weaver

Written by: Mark U.

As a child my first hero was John Wayne this came from watching his old movies with my grandfather. Dale became my second hero in 1987 I had always been a fan of Nascar since they used to show tape delay on ABC wide world of sports. But when I first so him race and just the way he carried himself he just reminded me of a cockier john Wayne. I have just been and still am a devoted fan.

That day was the worst day for myself and the rest of NASCAR and his family,we lost I think the last great American hero. Any way just to share a small story my wife and I were married on 4/29/95 on a cruise ship, that Sunday after *it was raining* we watched the Talladega race on the big screen TV in the bar * my wife's suggestion* and it just showed me that I really did marry the best woman in the world. This is also the woman who cried her eyes out when Dale won the Daytona 500 and cried with me the night he died. I don't think I will ever watch the races with as great a passion or interest again.

Mark U.

Written by: Shannon

My Dale Earnhardt story is a bit different. See I never got to meet Dale but I always wish I had. I started watching racing when I was about 10 years old at my grandparents home during my summer vacations. The one person they would always cheer for was Dale Earnhardt. I thought I would watch a race or two to see what it was all about and before long I was hooked. I am now a race fan for life. Dale always reminded me of my grandfather because my grandfather raced as well. He only raced for three years. His name was Marcel Emino, he too had car #3. So that number is pretty special to my family as well. He drove a 1939 Ford Coup. He built the car himself and maintained it. He raced for two straight years and then put the car in the dump. Then ten years later, he took it back out and race again! He only raced for that year then sold his race car to Junior Handly. My grandfather is a big race fan. Dale was his hero. He always said it amazed him how Dale would drive how he drove. My grandfather always wanted to meet Dale. We had planed to go several times to a race but never got the chance. I know Dale is watching, he will always be in our hearts. The #3 will live on forever.

Shannon

Written by: Monica Howser

The first time I saw Dale, I really met him, by that I mean that I was able to talk to him face to face. I was at a restaurant in Charlotte and it was about 1987. While I was having a bite to eat, I looked outside and I saw a man that looked like Dale get out of a Chevy truck. I was with my friend Diane and I told her to see if she thought it was Dale. She said it looked like Dale, but she wasn't sure. We could see that he was walking toward the door and was going to come inside. When he got inside he was given a seat over near a salad bar and he was also sitting with two more men. After getting a good look at Dale, I knew it was him. I thought before he started to eat that I would have time to speak with him before his food came. Diane and I both walked over to his table and spoke to Dale. He was very kind and nice to both of us, but was quiet and didn't seemed interested in talk to us. I know you aren't suppose to talk to a driver while he was eating, but he had not got his food yet. We could tell that we were bothering him and walked back to our seat. At that time I liked him and I understand why he didn't want to talk too much. That was my first time to ever see him up close. I went to about 3 or 4 races that year, it didn't take me long to know that Dale was not so nice at all. To tell the truth about it, he was the dirtiest driver I had ever seen. He acted like he owned the track and wanted ever other driver to know that I am going to win or I will wreck you. I got to the point that I started Booing him and sometimes I would wish that he would wreck, but not get hurt. The maddest that I ever got at Dale was at a race at Rockingham. I was a Bill Elliott fan and had been cheering for him ever since he won the money for the Winston Million. Bill was my favorite driver, but he was also my hero. During the race Bill was going to win, at least that is what I thought, but

137

Dale hit him so hard in the back bumper that he started spinning and went into the outside wall then slid down the track and hit the blocker wall at the pits. That was it and it was more than I could take, so from that day on I really hated Dale. I think he was the dirtiest driver that ever race and I was happy to see him go out of any race. You all know that he was killed at Daytona. I was watching the race on television when they said he had died. I felt sad in my heart, maybe out of guilt, but I didn't want him killed, but I still didn't like him. I hear people talk every day that are Dale fans and you hear them say, racing is not as much fun without Dale, I will have to agree with what they said, because it is true. They don't have as many wrecks as they use too. Dale caused 8 out of 10 of the wrecks, no wonder they miss him.

Written by: Hannah

I have just watched Dale Earnhardt's memorial service and cried just about the whole way through it. I wanted to tell you all about my greatest memory of Dale.

It was at the 1995 Brickyard 400. You all might not believe this, but I had money on the line for this race. I had drew Rusty Wallace out of a hat and I would win $43 if he won. I was cheering for him... but of course, Dale was leading. Rusty was in 2nd. Dale was my favorite. driver at that time, but I wanted that money so bad! The last lap of the race I said screw it and decided to root for Dale anyways. Who cares about the money! Dale went on to win and I went on to loose the money. If fact, my brother won it because he had Dale Earnhardt. Also his favorite. driver. When Dale came around for his victory lap, we were all so happy that he had won. Normally, after the race we all leave as soon as we can so we don't get held up in traffic.. but my brother and I did not want to leave. We didn't care if we got left behind (which would have been a big deal because I was 10 years old at the time and he was 11).. all we wanted to see was Dale come around in the pace car after he celebrated a bit. Sure enough, 10 or 15 minutes later here he came. We weren't the only ones in the stands, but the only ones in our area. When Dale got to where he could see us, we both put our thumbs up in the air and said "Good job Dale!".. he replied back "Thanks!" and flashed that great, unforgettable smile and gave us both a thumbs up! That was one of the greatest days of my life. There wasn't anyone or anything that could erase the smile off of our faces! That's the memory I want to remember Dale Earnhardt by. My most special race day ever. And one of his! ~Hannah~

Written by: Roger Erick

I am a fan for Sterling Marlin and I have been since he started racing. I like most of the drivers, but I don't like Dale Earnhardt because he is a poor sport and tries to wreck everybody to win the race. I don't hate him like some fans do, but I sure know a man that hates every gut in his body. I can't tell anything about me and Dale Earnhardt, because I don't hate him like some of the other fans. If you don't mind I will tell how much another fan that I know hates him. The fan's name was David, and I won't mention his last name. David always hated Dale Earnhardt. He hated him so much that every time you see David he always starts tell you how much he despises him. Down at our local Union 76 service station they were having a contest and all you had to do was just register for the prize. A different prize was given every week and you never knew what it would be until it was given away.

One Saturday a friend called and said that David had won the prize for this week. When David went down to get his prize, he found out that it was a big die cast car of Dale Earnhardt. The value of that car was about $70.00 if you had bought it in a hobby store. David hated Dale Earnhardt so much, that he laid the car under the back wheel of his truck and ran over it mashing it flat as a piece of cardboard. I don't see how anyone could be that much obsessed.

Written by: Brenda (aka BluePonie)

DALE, SR WAS THE MAN, THE INTIMIDATOR. HE WAS THE REASON FOR WATCHING SUNDAY AFTERNOON RACING. RICHARD PETTY MAY BE THE KING, BUT DALE, SR WILL ALWAYS BE THE MAN, IN MY EYES. HE KNEW HOW TO DRIVE AND GET TO THE TOP. HE HAD HIS OFF DAYS AND PROBLEMS JUST LIKE EVERYONE ELSE, BUT I LOVED TO WATCH HIM DRIVE. I JUST WISH WE WOULD HAVE HAD MORE YEARS TO GET TO WATCH HIM. I THINK HE JUST LOVED TO SHOW OFF SOMETIMES AND HE DID A GOOD JOB AT IT.

THANKS FOR LETTING ME SHARE MY OPINION AND KEEP ON STOMPIN THOSE RED WING BOOTS. NASCAR FOREVER YOUR FRIEND AND NASCAR BUDDY -

BRENDA (aka BluePonie)

GAMES YeeHawee Style

MIX AND MATCH YeeHawee Style

Please select the letter with its correct number.

1 Richard Petty
2 David Pearson
3 Cale Yarborough
4 Bobby Allison
5 Buddy Baker
6 Bobby Isaac
7 Charlie Glotzbach
8 Donnie Allison
9 Tiny Lund
10 Fred Lorenzen

A Hueytown
B Buck's son
C Hawaiian Tropic
D Golden Boy
E Charging
F Lynda
G Silver Fox
H Gentle Giant
I K and K Insurance
K Betty Jo

Please select the letter for it's correct number.
1 Dale Earnhardt
2 Rusty Wallace
3 Kenny Schrader
4 Jeff Burton
5 Terry Labonte
6 Bill Elliott

7 Ricky Rudd
8 Todd Bodine
9 Kevin Harvick
10 Sterling Marlin

A Paula
B Patti
C Kim
D Deanna
E Teressa
F Linda
G Diane
H Ann
I Cindy

Hint and Note: Only 9 women names are shown. Two drivers have a wife with the same name.

Please select the letter that matches the correct number.

1 Jeff Gordon
2 Ryan Newman
3 Kurt Busch
4 Jimmy Johnson
5 Kevin Harvick
6 Robby Gordon
7 Jamie McMurray
8 Bobby Labonte
9 Tony Stewart
10 Jeremy Mayfield

A 20
B 31
C 97
D 18

E 24
F 12
G 48
H 19
I 42
J 29

Please select the letter that matches the correct number.

1 Kyle Petty
2 Richard Childress
3 Rick Hendrick
4 Jack Roush
5 Robert Yates
6 Cal Wells
7 Roger Penske
8 Ray Everham
9 Beth Morganthal
10 Terry Bradshaw

A BAM
B Kerry Earnhardt
C # 2
D Sterling Marlin
E Dale Jarrett
F Mayfield and Elliott
G 24, 5 and 48
H Mark Martin
I RCR
J Victory Junction

THEN AND NOW YeeHawee Style

Shown below are some driver names and the the car number they drove in the 70's era. Who drove that car number in 2003?

David Pearson 21
Bobby Allison 22
Tiny Lund 16
Charlie Glotzbach 99
Pete Hamilton 40
Darrell Waltrip 88
Richard Petty 43
Richard Childress 3
Dick Hutchison 29
Bill Champion 10

Please choose the letter that matches the correct number.
1 Talladega
2 Daytona
3 Bristol
4 Darlington
5 North Wilksboro
6 Charlotte
7 Atlanta
8 Rockingham
9 Michigan
10 Dover

A Irish Hills
B World's Fastest Speedway
C Downs
D World's Center of Speed
E The Rock
F Highest Banks

G Richard Petty's Last Race
H Gone
I Too Tough to Tame
J The Hub of Racing

Please choose the letter that matches the correct number.

DRIVER
1 David Pearson
2 Donnie Allison
3 Buddy Baker
4 Bobby Allison
5 Bobby Isaac
6 Fireball Roberts
7 Fred Lorenzen
8 Darrell Waltrip
9 Harry Gant
10 LeeRoy Yarbrogh

CAR OWNER
A Junior Johnson
B Hoss Ellington
C Wood Brothers
D Bert and Hal
E Ray Fox
F Diegard
G Holman and Moody
H Smokey Yunick
I Roger Penske
J K and K Insurance

Shown below are scrambled letter for a drivers last name. Please name the driver.

1 nonseb
2 hnojson
3 alcwael
4 handtraed
5 aneotbl
6 aeimflyd
7 aersrhd
8 taetrjr
9 wnmena
10 cresnep

ANSWERS BY CODE (2003)

1 If Jeff Gordon was #20, Tony Stewart was #16, Mark Martin was #2. What number would Jeff Burton be?

2 Who drives the square root of 25?

3 How much is Bobby Labonte plus Kyle Petty plus Bill Elliott.

4 If car numbers were dollars how much money would Jack Roush have for 2003?

5 If you add Caterpillar plus Dupont plus Viagra, what would the total be?

6 If Rusty Wallace, Terry Labonte, Michael Waltrip and Sterling Marlin were all together as partners. One driver got mad and leaves. Which driver left if the total was 60 after he was gone?

7 If car numbers could be over a 100 and you were going to drive a car # equal to the total of Jeff Burton, Ricky Rudd, Kurt Busch and Bill Elliott. What would the car # be?

8 If Johnny Benson drove # 5, Tony Stewart drove # 10, Sterling Marlin drove #20, what # would Dale Earnhardt, Jr. drive?

9 I went to the concession stand to buy some food. The total for all the food was Jeremy Mayfield, Kenny Schrader, Kevin Harvick, Robby Gordon and Brett Bodine. How much did the food cost?

10 Name a driver who's number was twice the # of Tony Stewart.

The year is 2003. Who is the best driver today of the ones paired together?

1 Jeff Gordon or Ryan Newman.
2 Rusty Wallace or Terry Labonte.
3 Johnny Benson or Rickey Craven.
4 Jimmy Johnson or Kevin Harvick.
5 Kyle Petty or Kenny Schrader.
6 Matt Kenseth or Dale Earnhardt, Jr.
7 Tony Stewart or Kurt Busch.
8 Rickey Rudd or Elliott Sadler.
9 Dale Jarrett or Bobby Labonte.
10 Jeff Green or Steve Park.

The year is 2003. Who is the best?
1 WC Driver.
2 TV announcer.
3 Crew chief.
4 Sponsor
5 Car owner.
6 Engine Builder.
7 Multi car owner
8 Radio announcer.
9 Track owner.
10 Track promoter.

If you could go to one of the two races at the tracks paired together, which would it be.

1 Talladega or Daytona
2 Bristol or Richmond
3 Texas or Las Vegas
4 Darlington or Rockingham
5 Watkins Glen or Sonoma
6 Charlotte or Atlanta
7 Bristol or Brickyard 400
8 Martinsville or New Hampshire
9 Dover or Michigan
10 Chicago or Kansas.

Here is a bonus question. Of all the tracks listed above, which one is your favorite?

Please fill in the blanks to spell a driver's name for 2003.
1 ____o___g_
2 ____e_h
3 ____i_k
4 __r_e__
5 _o___o_
6 ___w_o_
7 ___u___y
8 ___d_e_
9 s___n__
10 ___i___n

Please fill in the blank to make a paragraph.

I went to Charlotte and the first person I saw was W_____. He was tailing with another driver ___i_t_. They were talking about the pole and was wondering who would get the pole. One said it would be __r_o_ and the

148

other driver said it would be __w_a_. While going through inspection __e__r_ was found to be illegal, but his buddy ___o__e had no problem at all. Everyone was surprised that day to see __r_i_ win the post and __h__d__ on the outside pole. When the race started the first driver to jump out front was __r_I__. However when the checker flag fell the winner was _e__ __r__n.

Choose the letter that has the opposite meaning for the number.

1 Race Car
2 Winner
3 Five Hundred Miles
4 Loose
5 Overweight
6 Marbles
7 Ball of Fire
8 Rain
9 Turn two
10 Asphalt

A Turn four
B Looser
C Concrete
D Zero
E Tractor trailer
F Tight
G Light
H Clean track
I Dry
J Bucket of water

Who am I?

1 I am middle aged. I live in Tennessee. My dad was a race driver. My mother is named Eula Faye.

2 I have been married and divorced. I am now dating. I lived in Californie, Indiana and Florida.

3 I am a young driver. I am not in WC yet, but my brother is a WC driver. My brother has big ears. He is not much older than me.

4 I am a very short driver. I love the Marines.

5 I am the youngest of three racing brothers that are all 3 driving at this time. My first name begins with a M.

6 I have a daughter named Star and a son named Chase.

7 My daddy drives the Viagra #6, what is my name?

8 My name is Danny and I drive sprint cars for Tony Stewart.

9 I am married to Rusty Wallace.

10 My brother is Ward

WHO AM I? PART 2

1 I own Sterling Marlins car.

2 I use to be crew chief for Davy Allison, but I am a car owner now.

3 One of my favorite drivers was killed in a plane crash just before trying to land at Bristol.

4 I was he one hat told Richard Childress to retire from driving and hire Dale Earnhardt to drive the # 3.

5 I was sponsored, by Peidemont Airlines, Sunoco, Budweiser and Kellogs.

6 My mother's name is Annie. My daddy was called Big Bill.

7 I was the crew chief for DW when he ran his first race at Talladega.

8 I am one of the youngest drivers on the circuit and I will be driving for Rick Hendrick in 2004.

9 I won 105 races and have silver hair.

10 I was the first driver to win the Winston Million.

WHO AM I? PART 3

1 Some people call me Buffet Benny

2 I was killed in a helicopter crash at Talladega.

3 I was know as a lover boy and died with Aids.

4 I was called handsome Harry.

5 My wife's name is Judy. I call my daddy Pops.

6 I was killed at Riverside and Curtis was my best friend.

7 My son is known as THE KING in racing.

8 My name was not Fireball. So who am I.

9 I was given my nickname because I wore big round and thick glasses.

10 I use to own the #3 car driven by Buddy Baker, Charlie Glotzbach, David Pearson and Junior Johnson. My last name is a animal.

I hope you enjoyed these games. If you have any questions, comments or would like to know the answers, please email me at pettychamp@webtv.net

My FRIENDS Yeehawee Style

"ONE TOUGH DUDE, David R. Porter"

Written by: By David R. Porter   PureWCup~Dave R.P.

This actually occurred in the spring of 2002. It was about a NASCAR fans big dream of meeting a bunch of his good buddies at the Talladega Winston Cup race. That old campgrounds was starting to look like heaven. What more could you ask for than the big race with good friends over the hillbilly grill. Had the ticket and all the plans when the bad news came. It was a visit to the doctors office and some routine tests. The doc said very calmly that I had four blockages and would require a quadruple bypass. That's straight to the heart of the matter and has nothing to do with exhaust pipes. It was decision time and if I was going to make that race it had to be done now. It took 2-3 days to get checked into Wake Med and have my chest laid open. Ten days later the operation was complete, the tubes and oxygen were removed and a shock treatment was done to get the old heart back in rhythm. It was five days until the race and I had to get clearance from that doc. After all he had told me that the best thing to do was take walks every day to get my strength back. He knew how bad I wanted to get to Talladega and this is what he told my wife. We don't want your husband to be cutting the lawn, vacuuming the house or washing any dishes but he can go to the race if he takes it easy. Well I checked out those scars down the middle of my chest and up my left leg and said I don't feel a thing. It was only a little over 500 miles down to Talladega about the same distance as a good race. I can do that. Well I loaded up the Grand Prix GT, tossed in the sleeping bag and goodies and hit the road. Shined up the car right down to it's special license plate. It's one of those vanity things and reads, PUREWCUP, North Carolina. and that's a fact. Have you ever been to Talladega? Well it's one danged big place. It seemed like I walked a hundred miles that weekend. Well I had a great time with Omer, Champ, Bob and Ron Perkins, Charles (Mac Man) and the gang. We yeehawee'd around the old hillbilly grill and they told me, "Man you are one tough dude". Only five days after heart surgery? How bad have you got it?

WRONG TURN LEADS TO JEFF GORDON

Written by: Sue, upstate New York

My husband and I are huge NASCAR fans. Our favorite driver is Jeff Gordon. We got to met Jeff Gordon in 1997 at Atlanta the Napa 500 the last race of the season. But that weekend almost didn't happen. We live UP State NY,We woke up early Saturday looked out and it was snowing real bad. Our flight out of Steward airport was at 8am.The 45 min trip to Steward took us 2 hours. We checked in at 7.15am to be told there was a 3 hour delay. Sat down and had breakfast and got seats by the window, it didn't stop snowing, it looked really bad outside. I was getting very upset, and more delays. At 1pm all flights out of Steward were canceled, no flights out that day. We were about to leave for home, broken heart and all, when they announce they will have a few buses to take us to Kennedy airport, My husband and I ran to catch the bus. Nothing but NASCAR fans on the bus. We had lots of fun on our trip down. most of the fans already had too much to drink. We arrived at Kennedy at 4pm. very happy to get new flight out, because there was a chance we would not leave at all. We took off at 5pm, stopover at Ohio and NC. Arrived in Atlanta 10pm. Got our rental car and headed for Days inn 10 hrs late, they had given our room out, we forgot to call and let them know we would be late.

Did get a small room thank God, all we want was sleep so that was ok. Woke up Sunday morning put the news on, to find out Jeff Gordon had crashed his car at practice in happy hour, he was cleaning his tires and he spun into Bobby Hamilton's car and crashed both cars, it was frost on the tack,they had to go to the back 33rd 34th. Jeff Gordon was going for his 2nd Championship and had to finish 20th or better. Lot of nerves JG fans that Sunday. We got to the track early, it was so cold.30° at the track. We were told it would be nice and warm in GA in November and we didn't need heavy coats. WRONG.! All we had was thin windbreakers on. Had to laugh at our self, all the fans came dressed in snowmobile suits, hunting outfits gloves scarf hats, hot coffee in thermos bottles. No beers that day. When we got to our seat it was frost on them. We made a few trips to see the Winston folks, they were handing out free face towels,we made pillows out of them. The temperature did go up, and the race was on. I was very worried for Jeff all day, his backup car was not to fast, but he end up 17th 3 lap down and won the Championship by 14 points over Dale Jerrett. Bobby Labonte won the race. It was a exciting race, and I don't think I sat down in my seats at all, didn't need the pillows. Next morning NASCAR had breakfast for the Champions at the track. All the fans could get free breakfast and meet the Champions, Jeff Gordon and Randy Lajoie. Randy had won the Busch Champion. There was so many fans we couldn't get near the stage to get Jeff's autograph. I was heart broken. Our flight to NY was at 3pm, so we had a few hours to kill. We decided to take our car on the track. For $25 you could take your car and drive 3 laps. It was exciting and fun, but I was still very disappointed I didn't meet Jeff Gordon. On our way out of the track my husband made a left turn instead of right. We were just driving and checking out everything, and there was this beautiful motor home with lots of Nascar fans, especially Jeff Gordon fans hanging out. And there was Jeff Gordon signing autographs. He was trying to leave, but the fans got to him first...THANK GOD. Jeff was so nice and polite. We got our pictures taken with him, and 3 autographs each. I was the happiest person in the world. The weekend was perfect. We had the best time.

We go to 56 races a year, and always have a good time. Bristol is our favorite track,and there is were we meet Omer and Champ every August.

~~#24FAN~~

By Jean Cawthon

Much has been much said about Dale Earnhardt. Some call him the Intimidator because of his style on the track. Others call him the man in black, some have cursed him, others have praised him. It has often been said that you either love him, or you hate him. Regardless of which it may be, everyone respects him. My first real memories of Dale Earnhardt in NASCAR were back in his rookie year. He came on as a brash, cocky driver, who would not hesitate to rub fenders or do a little bump drafting if it would get him to the front. To many, he was too aggressive. Still, he finished as Rookie of the Year. The next year he would take his first championship. Over the next few years, the number of fans who would idolize Dale would grow. Almost as fast were the number of race fans who would criticize him. There were also those drivers who did not always have nice things to say after a race. I remember vividly several of the races where Dale and Rusty would bang on each other until one or the other wrecked, or decided to pit. Some say that the scene from "Days of Thunder" where Bill France is coming down hard on the the two drivers was based on an actual incident where Mr. France called Dale and Rusty in. Being a Rusty Wallace fan, I hated it every time I saw Dale get near. I always wondered who would end up in the wall, or if both would end up with a DNF.

I soon realized though that both drivers were enjoying the excitement. They had come to expect it from each other, and were glad to give the fans a show. In later years, Dale and Rusty would become very close friends. Instead of the old bump and grind, they would often hook up and make a run for the front. They still loved racing each other, but they also knew that on a good day, they could be a heck of a team. Although I have always been a Ford fan, I soon found myself liking Dale and his style. Many would be the times that I would cheer him on. Like so many others, I too had been touched by the legend. At the last summer race at Talladega, I remember standing under a tarp in the rain watching as the drivers flew in to the local airport. One by one they came in, King Richard, Dale, Rusty, and so many others. We had a long wait that day for the race. After several rain delays, the race finally started. It was 68 degrees on a July afternoon, and many of us looked like drowned rats. It didn't matter though, because we were there to enjoy the fun. About half way through the race, Dale and Ernie Irvin were running up front. Dale had spent a good part of the afternoon in the top ten, and the crowd was on their feet as he took the lead and showed what he could do. Next thing I remember is seeing his car go into the catch fence in the tri-oval.

For quite a while, many of us sat in silence, wondering, is he alright, is he hurt. Finally, the word got around, he had some injuries, but was fine. This would be the start of his long winless streak. During this long streak, many would wonder, can he still do it, is he scared, is it time to retire. The answer came at Daytona in February of '98. The one race that had eluded him finally became his. The post-race celebration was one of the largest ever, with crews lining up on pit row to congratulate the "Man in Black". It would be his only win that year. The next year he would win 3 races, and in 2000 he would win two, including one of best Talledega races ever. As the 2001 season opened up, Dale had much to be happy about. He had three cars in his DEI stable, RCR was ready for a new year, and the announcement had been made that Childress would add a third car the next year. Although a Twin 125 win would not be had this year, Dale was still in good spirits. Sunday, February 18th, 2001.

I remember well the shots of Dale walking down pit row before the race. His arm around Teresa, his son saying something to bring a smile to dad's face. As Dale went on down pit row, he would stop and talk to Michael Waltrip. He would continue on stopping to talk with several other drivers before finally coming to his car. Before getting in the car, Dale turned and gave Teresa a kiss and hug. As the race came into the closing laps, Dale was sitting in a position to see a sight that would make anyone happy.

His son and a dear friend were running one and two. On the last lap, it was evident that DEI would get it's first Daytona 500 with the boss finishing right behind them. What happened next and how it happened is something that will be talked about for years.

Sadly, no one will ever know the truth.

WATKINS GLEN

Written by: Stereo Steve

Thanks for the invite to get in the book. Really don't have a story about the guys you mentioned. I have seen them at the glen in many different cars, I think even Johnny Rutherford raced a sedan there once.

The interesting' thing 'bout the "glen" occurs durin' one car qualifyin'. As you know, one cannot see most of the track so you hear the sounds as the car runs it's lap. When a star such as DE of JG goes around you can hear the car an' actually hear the boos change to cheers an' back to boos again, as the car passes different parts of the track. I always assumed that it doesn't sound the same at a circle track. thanks again. - ss

Written by: C. M. Cunningham

Omer when I found out about your book I wanted to be in it, but I can't write much of a story. I will tell some things that I like about Nascar races.
1 I like it because the cars are like the ones we drive and are not handmade.
2 The drivers are easier to talk to than in most other divisions.
3 I like the big tracks like Daytona and Talladega. I am a speed demon.
4 Bristol is my favorite short track.
5 My favorite driver is Jeff Gordon
6 My favorite track is Daytona.
7 My favorite driver is Kevin Harvick
8 I don't like Kurt Bush.
9 I don't like Jimmy Spencer, but he is a tough driver.
10 Jeff Gordon reminds me of Richard Petty.

11 Matt Kenseth reminds me of David Pearson.
12 I like to see the jets fly over the speedway.
13 I like to camp when I go to the races.
14 Richard Childress is my favorite team owner.
15 I like DW more than the rest of the tv people.

Written by: Jason Whitaker

The best time I have ever had in my life was the time that me and two of my buddies went to Darlington and stayed the weekend in the infield. The place was jammed packed and everyone was touching elbows. If you want to party, that is the place to be. We went into the infield on Friday and didn't come out until after the race was finished on Sunday. All of us partied and never slept the whole weekend. We sure paid for it when we did straighten up some. I was about dead, but it was worth it. I didn't even know who won the race until I got back home.

One of these days I am going to get a good seat in the grandstand and really see a race. Everyone says it is good and I can't wait to stay sober and see what I have missed. Omer, I always said you should write a book because I have read your stories on the Internet and they are better than any I have read in a book.
Written by: Jess Webb

When I was a little kid, I wanted to see Richard Petty. I started going to the races when I was 10 years old. Now I am 42 years old. Here is the story.

When I started going to the races when I was 10 years old I became a Richard Petty fan right off the bat. He was a class act and I sure thought he was cool. For several years I tried to be able to talk to Richard or at least have him sign a autograph for me. Richard would always stay at the race tracks for hours and sign autographs for the fans. Every race I went to I wanted to stay and git his famous signature, but my dad wanted to head home to beat the traffic. As I begin to get older I was still trying to be able to talk with Richard, but that day never came until I had a terrible wreck in my truck when I was 32 years old. That wreck left me paralyzed from my neck down. I was bedfast or in a wheelchair for the rest of my wife. I remained in the hospital for several months before being released. I had to go back to visit my doctor each month. When I went to the hospital for one of my visits, I fell upon the happiest day of my life. You see, our hospital has a special unit for crippled children. On the day I was there a nurse told me that Richard Petty was down stairs to visit the children. She and lots of others at the hospital knew I was Richard's best fan. I told the nurse to put me in the wheelchair and take me down there to see Richard. She didn't want to disrupt what she was doing because she had me all hooked up and in traction. I didn't care what the problem was I had waited almost 20 years to see Richard and nothing was going to stop me now. I sure didn't know that behind my back the nurse and others at the hospital had made arrangements for Richard to come and see me.

After about a hour, my nurse walked in and said, Jess someone is here to see you. There he was, Richard Petty smiling like a opossum when he walked over to me. I started crying because I waited so long for this. Richard said he heard I was his fan and wanted to meet me. He was so nice and talked about me being all hooked to all of those hospital things. He said that is the way I look when I am in my race car.

Richard stayed with me about 15 minutes and when he started to leave, he took off his belt, buckled it around my neck, and said I needed some more things hooked up to me and he said don't hang yourself and walked away leaving me his belt as a gift for me.

I am a poor person and never have any extra money, but as bad as I need money, I would not sell Richard's belt for ten thousand dollars.

Written By: ROADAPPLE RICK from California

Hi Omer I didn't know what to say if you want to use this you can your buddy RICK.

I like to tell you how I met my good friend Omer. I was trying to find some new friends I went to the new group it is where I met my good friend Omer he made me feel welcome he is a really nice person he is always trying to help some one we need more people like him.

Alan Kulwicki "MY WAY"

Written by: My special buddy, Stan-Fan from Florida.

There was a sad, lonely, melancholy face to Alan Kulwicki, probably brought on by the loss of his mother at an early age. The native Wisconsin driver, who for years had clawed, scraped, and managed to cling to the outer rim of stock car racing's premier Winston Cup circuit, never with major sponsorship, except a short stint with Zerex Antifreeze, would, in 1992, pull an amazing and improbable surprise run at the Winston Cup Championship. Coupled with crew-chief Paul Andrews, and the emergence of the Ford Thunderbird as a competitive race car, Kulwicki, along with a fan favorite, family racer, Davey Allison, would emerge in a fight to the finish, against a legendary driver, and champion, Bill Elliott. That the two former driver's, Kulwicki and Allison would share the same terrible fate of death in the air, a year after their tremendous runs, was unimaginable at the start of the 1992 season. NASCAR fans were "all a glitter" at the racing marriage of famed, "good ol-boy" stock car original driver-owner, Junior Johnson's merger with Winston Cup Champion, and Most Popular Driver, Bill Elliott, under Budweiser sponsorship, for a run at the title. Few doubted that the Johnson-Elliott merger wouldn't produce a head table visit at New York's Waldorf Astoria Hotel at the end of the year, and it would almost happen. In fact, it was so close, the two, Elliott and Kulwicki, could have shared champagne from the same head table bottle. That inscrutable face of Alan Kulwicki, however, hid a "mechanic's brain" with a single-minded passion for success that literally bordered on obsession. The former Winston Cup Rookie of The Year, who was driver-owner-businessman of his team, coupled with another "motorhead" crew-chief Paul Andrews, who together probably could have been Vice-President's of Ford Motor Company in the Engineering Division, were a perfect match.

Years of learning, scraping, tooling, re-tooling of his race car's, learning everything he could from mechanics, drivers, and any source that would assist him on his quest for success, all came home to roost in a memorable and delightful NASCAR season in 1992. Tired of running second fiddle to the "Bow-Tie" Chevrolet set, Ford Motor Company had a competitive race car in the Ford Thunderbird.

Alan Kulwicki finally received major sponsorship, when most red-blooded males favorite Southern restaurant, Hooter's, came aboard to sponsor his Number 7. The Ford Thunderbird he and Paul Andrews rolled out of the barn for the 1992 season, was if nothing else, wickedly fast. The tone of the season would be set in the second race, in chilly Richmond, Virginia, on a tough

162

little D-shaped 3/4-mile oval track, as Alan Kulwicki and Bill Elliott would duel to the finish, slamming together on the final turn, enough to leave a clear tire imprint on Elliott's winning Budweiser car, as the crowd roared and cheered the famous Georgia star to Victory Lane. In the pits, physically and emotionally, after the race, Alan Kulwicki, speaking of his second place, one-foot loss to Bill Elliott that day, replied sadly, "We'll be back, we'll be back." And back he would come, in a memorable season which would have historic implications for stock car racing. With a win at Bristol Motor Speedway's first race of that season, a track which he ran with success, and another later in the season at Pocono in Pennsylvania, Kulwicki was competitive throughout, but found himself 278 points behind the second generation, richly sponsored, driver-star, Davey Allison, and his Number 28 Texaco Havoline, Ford Thunderbird machine. Alan however, would storm back into contention for the title.

A Davey Allison's victory at Phoenix in the second-to-last race of the season, set the popular Alabama driver up for his first of what many expected Winston Cup Championship's to come, as the tour headed to the finale at Atlanta Motor Speedway, "Awesome Bill From Dawsonville" country. Allison, Kulwicki, Elliott and Harry Gant, all had chances to win the title at Atlanta in a race which featured NASCAR's greatest legend, Richard Petty appearing in his final race, and soon to become, marquee-idol and champion, Jeff Gordon's first race on the senior circuit. Roaring around Atlanta's high-banked curves, Allison, Elliott and Kulwicki dueled throughout the afternoon, with Allison keeping the title in sight all the way. However, Davey would tangle with the speedy Kodak-sponsored machine of Ernie Irvan, and the ensuing wreck would eliminate his chance for the win, leaving Elliott and Kulwicki to race on into the afternoon, and history. And race he did. With a craftiness suitable to the Hooter's Owl emblem on the hood of his Number 7, Alan Kulwicki would duel Bill Elliott the rest of the way home, getting every single ounce of power and performance from his race car. The famous Elliott would eventually win the Atlanta race, but Alan Kulwicki, the "Underbird" having dropped the T-emblem from his Ford Thunderbird as his motto of underdog, would lead the most laps, and gain the five bonus points, to defeat Bill Elliott for the 1992 Winston Cup Championship by that margin. The always gentleman racer, Bill Elliott replied in the pit road interview, "We won but we lost," as a delighted Alan Kulwicki did what would become a famous backward "Polish Victory Lap" to celebrate his improbable Winston Cup Championship win, with crew-chief Paul Andrews basking in the reflected glory of their surprising win. "We'll be back" Alan had said at Richmond earlier in the season. That he would be back all the way to the championship, few could believe, and that he and his fellow racing competitor Davey Allison wouldn't be back long, would cast a terrible pall on the ensuing season.

As the famous Frank Sinatra song ~My Way~ was played at the NASCAR awards banquet at the Waldorf-Astoria Hotel highlighting his championship accomplishment, Alan Kulwicki would say. "I want to be as good a champion as I can be in case the chance never happens again." The "God's Of Racing" are generous and cruel. In 1992, the moon and stars aligned perfectly for a wonderful championship season from three of the finest driver's ever to grace the NASCAR senior circuit, Alan Kulwicki, Davey Allison and Bill Elliott. On April 1, 1993, the famous "Man-In-Black" champion Dale Earnhardt, Senior, the one driver nobody ever would have expected to die in a racecar, would learn from his pilot, on approach to Bristol, Tennessee, that Alan Kulwicki and his entourage had died when their corporate airplane crashed in the Tennessee hills. At Bristol Motor Speedway, Earnhardt, and the entire drivers, and crews of the Winston Cup family, including Davey Allison, himself to die a short time later that year in a helicopter accident at Talladega, Alabama, stood in silent tribute to NASCAR's short-lived 1992 champion's memory, as the Hooters race hauler slowly circled the track in silent memory of Alan Kulwicki, the "Underbird."

GIVE AWARDS CEREMONY A SHAKE UP

By: Stacy Sawyer speedwaymedial.com

Even though nearly a year has passed since last year's Winston Cup Series Award Ceremony, I am still able to laugh about what a fiasco it turned out to be. For those of you that missed it, do you think of flying acrobats when you think of NASCAR? Or do you think of James Woods as a NASCAR spokesman? Well last year, that is part of the reason TNT's award show was highly criticized and may go down in history as worst show ever. For many fans, the award ceremony is highly anticipated and helps ease the ache many feel during the dreaded off-season. Hopefully this year the producers are working hard to make sure that Winston's last Award Ceremony will be able to reflect the quality NASCAR fans have come to expect. I'll never be able to fully understand the reasoning that went on to pick James Woods to host last year's event. It only makes sense that TNT would choose someone like Alan Bestwick or Benny Parsons to emcee this year's show. A less obvious choice might be the pit reporters. Actually, it's the pit reporters that probably know the drivers and their crews better than the boys in the booth. The only reason I have come up with for the flying acrobats was the producers thought the drivers' speeches would not provide enough entertainment to hold an audience for the entire show. That is more than a reasonable conclusion. Increasingly, drivers' speeches have become thank you letters to their sponsors. There is nothing wrong with thanking their sponsors; it's the sponsors that helped them achieve their goals. Sometimes I think the sponsors don't realize the more the driver looks like a mouthpiece the more turned off fans become.

One speech that still stands out from last year is Tony Stewart's. Tony's relationship with the press last year was tumultuous to say the least. Before he began his speech he started taking pictures of the press. Whether it was a peace offering or a taunt, the moment was truly entertaining.

This year, I'm looking to the drivers to make this ceremony the best ever. All of them need to throw away the model of a teleprompter speech. One way to shake things up would be to let their crew play a part. Let's face it, the drivers are nothing without a top-notch crew. I've found it insulting that on award night the champion's pit crew can look forward to a few camera shots. Considering all the commercials the drivers have made, they should go to Hollywood and put together a mini movie with their crew to show how they were able to beat the competition. Another idea might be to make a music video. Did any of you catch Sean Pragano's hot country song that featured hi-lights and low-lights of the 2003 season on Totally NASCAR? Pragano should offer up his expertise to any driver who is struggling to come up with ideas. This is also a great merchandise opportunity. I hail from Chicago, and back in 1986 there was no hotter video than the Chicago Bears performing Super Bowl Shuffle. The key to this idea working is that the driver and crew are the stars. It won't work if there is a popular band doing the

166

singing or if the crew featured is a bunch of actors. It has to be authentic.

The two drivers I'm looking forward to hearing from the most are Bill Elliott and Terry Labonte. I'm hoping they will be the most creative. It would be cool to see Elliott do something with his son Chase. I remember hearing during one of the races something about Chase wanting to either have 20 as a car number or something along those lines. Maybe Elliott could do a short film of a recurring nightmare with the press and his disillusioned fans hounding him about his future plans. Labonte could make light of the fact that he has avoided all the nonsense. Most importantly, Bill Elliott and Dale Earnhardt, Jr. have to be a part of the decision making process for the presentation of most popular driver. It would be nice to see Elliott be the presenter. Either way, I hope the point comes across that there are no conspiracies or ill will. Finally, something better come of the Big Apple Sweepstakes we've been hearing about since the Chevy Rock & Roll 400 at Richmond International Raceway.

T.J. Timmons from Peabody, Mass. won a trip to New York and is supposed to be a special correspondent at the ceremony. As often as they talked about this promotion, I hope Timmons gets to have some fun and appears on TV more than just once. If TNT, NBC and NASCAR.com do something like this again, they really should have given more then one trip away. What if Timmons is camera shy? There were 10 different races that viewers had a chance to send in an entry. There should have been 10 different winners, and then there could have been a contest to see who would make the best correspondent. Honestly, has reality TV taught these people nothing? Even Winston's No Bull program gave 5 different people a chance, and they were giving away one million dollars.

Award shows today are a dime a dozen. It's a pretty safe bet that diehard fans are going to watch the ceremony despite the entertainment magnitude, but for viewers just tuning in it's a great opportunity for NASCAR and its drivers to showcase why their fans are so passionate about the sport they love.

- Stacy Sawyer speedwaymedia.com

DAVEY'S SPIRIT STILL LIVES ON IN OUR FAMILY

Lynne, Matt & Chris Gregory

A Davey Allison Tribute by DieHard Yates Fans
http://personal.cfw.com/~racin/Davey_Allison.htm

Chris turned 9 in November of 1993 and his birthday party was a celebration dedicated to Davey's memory. His cake was decorated with the 28 Texaco Havoline Car and his present was a Davey Allison jacket. For Christmas we bought an ornament with Davey's picture on it and every year it hangs on our tree in his memory ...along with a photo ornament of Chris and Davey. And our 1993 Christmas card was Chris and Davey's picture and the words embossed on it were "Silent Night"... that seemed to sum up our racing year.

The Winston Cup Wives Auxiliary published a racing cookbook and in it were the recipes of Davey's favorite pre-race meal. We have made this and enjoyed it, and have included all 4 recipes so you can make the meal too. Lynne's Mother made a memorial grape vine wreath trimmed in Texaco Havoline colors which hangs on our front door even today. And when our family was requested to make a quilt square describing our family for a 1997 family reunion quilt... ours was a 28 quilt square.

Lynne still wears the shirt she had air brushed to her specifications in Davey's honor. She has commercial licensed shirts but wanted hers to be a one of a kind one to be her special tribute to Davey. Matt carries the license plate RYR RACN and Davey decals on one of our vehicles. Yes, Davey's spirit lives on with us. We were fortunate. We got to meet him for a brief moment in time, and it is forever etched in our minds. Chris summed it up best when, shortly after Davey's death, he said "Davey will always live on in our hearts." Children know exactly how to say what adults sometimes can't put into words.

THE WORSE RACING NEWS WE HAVE EVER HEARD

Monday July12th arrived and we were still flyin' high with Davey's great finish. At the end of the workday, one of Lynne's friends stopped by to tell her that she heard Davey's plane had gone down and that's all she knew. We frantically called the local radio station and they confirmed what Lynne had been told...that Davey, piloting his new helicopter, crashed in the infield of Talladega Super speedway that day. When we got home and told Chris, he burst into tears as Lynne had done earlier. We kept calling the radio station where Matt had worked as an announcer at one time. They shared the updates they had....He had flown about 60 miles with Red Farmer accompanying him to watch Neil Bonnett's son David practice. His helicopter was only a few feet away from a safe landing when it shot 25 feet up into the air. It spun counterclockwise, rolled and crashed with the tail rotor striking a fence on the way down. The news on his condition was not very promising. We went to bed knowing Davey was a fighter and praying for a miracle.

169

When we awoke Tuesday morning the news was still bleak. For 16 hours we waited to hear good news...it never came. That morning, on Lynne's Dad's birthday, our worst fear was realized....Davey was no longer with us on this earth. He had gone to a better place and left us with a tremendous void and pain in our hearts. We, the fans, and the racing community were numb again. (a detailed story here from Stock Car Racing Magazine) Red Farmer was with Davey that fateful day. (picture of Davey, Red & Bobby) We had lost the great Alan Kulwicki, 1992 Winston Cup Champion, (photo is our autographed trading card) just three months earlier in a plane crash on April 1st. The Allison's had lost son Clifford on August 13th 1992 with the practice accident at Michigan. Now this. How could we continue following our sport when we just lost our personal champion?

THE FIRST TIME WE EVER MET DAVEY, LIVE AND IN PERSON

On Mar. 3, 1993 (the Wednesday before the Sunday Richmond race) Lynne called the Leo's who ran Davey's fan club where we were members. She was trying to find out where Davey might be doing any personal appearances in Virginia. They connected her with Robert Yates Racing where her call was promptly and cheerfully returned with the information needed to surprise Chris. On Thurs. Mar. 4, 1993 it was raining, sleeting and ice was everywhere. In spite of this "wintery mix", Lynne left work early to pick up Chris from school to drive 1 1/2 hours to Richmond. They arrived at 5:00 after driving through horrible weather. The 28 car was in front of Track Auto (picture at right). We could actually look under the hood of the car. That's when Chris finally realized why they had driven to Richmond...he was so excited when he was told that he would actually meet Davey. We were 13th in line to see Davey, and the line grew and grew! At 7:20 we got what we came for...to speak to Davey for a brief moment in time. Chris gave him a picture of the 28 he had drawn and gave him a huge hug!

Lynne was snapping pictures but was delighted to see how warmly Davey responded to our son. She shook Davey's hand and was impressed that he made sincere eye contact with her and each fan who followed. He signed hats for Chris and Lynne and when she explained why she desperately needed her husband's hat signed too (limit one item to be autographed per person) he willing did that one too. Although he was unshaven and looked exhausted... he was still a champion in our eyes and ever so cheerful, joking and smiling. His smile told us that we, the fans, were important. You may be wondering why Matt was not with us. He had a meeting that had been scheduled prior to finding out where Davey would be and was not able to come...or so Chris and I thought. At the very last minute, he canceled the meeting and then drove almost 2 1/2 hours to try to catch us in line so he too could see Davey! As fate would have it, he saw our car in the parking lot, but missed seeing us since we were at the front of the line. But at least he too got to see Davey. Matt says he felt compelled to go...and is so glad he did. He just stood there and enjoyed watching Davey interact with the fans awhile before he drove home. Davey qualified 14th and went on win that Sunday March 7 at Richmond. He was happy (photo source unknown) in Victory Lane! Little did we know at the time that would be his last win.

DOWN IN HUEYTOWN

The following article was written by a very good friend of mine.

By Staff Columnist Joe Ewert www.teamdei.net

The summer of 2002 was one I will never forget. My dad took me, my sister, and my girlfriend on a week-long voyage through the South. Our first stop was in Fort Smith, Arkansas to visit good ol' Red Dog. He took us in for a night and showed us the best darn pig roast you can imagine. From Arkansas, we ventured to Memphis, Tennessee to visit Graceland. It was closed for the day so, disappointed, we vowed to come back before we headed home. From there it was a long trek to Talladega, Alabama, and you can only imagine what we went there for! The track is absolutely amazing. The tour we went on took us into the track and the turns are steep enough to make your butt clench. The Motorsports Hall of Fame was something dreamlike. Seeing the very last car Alan Kulwicki raced, to seeing the Bobby and Davey Allison cars that finished first and second in the Daytona 500, all the cars there just took my breath away. They even had some wrecked cars on display to show the carnage that our great sport can dish out. The first was Ricky Craven's 41 car that flipped into the fence in 1996. Another was Neil Bonnett's 31 Goodwrench car that rolled a few times, and the worst was Michael Waltrip's Busch car that disintegrated at Bristol. But while the Talladega trip was something to remember, the next and final stop in Alabama was the kind of thing that you will tell your grandkids about one day. Destination: Hueytown.

For me, having my dad get in the rental car, look at me and simply say, "Hueytown," was all I needed. I felt like a little kid, and I'm sure a lot of people that read this will understand this feeling of anticipation and sheer joy at its very best. For those of you who wonder what Hueytown is, it is the home of Allison racing. The Alabama Gang was born in Florida, but moved to Alabama which was the hot spot of racing at that time.

The history behind this incredible place just rings throughout the streets all the way to Allison-Bonnett Memorial Drive.

The following is a story that will stick in my mind as the highlight to one of the greatest vacations I've ever had. Unsure of where the shop was, my dad pulled into a body shop and I asked where the Bobby Allison shop was. The guy looked at me, smiled and said, "The shop? Heck I'll tell ya where that S.O.B. lives!" Upon getting my directions I hopped back in and told my dad. The shop was at the end of a dead-end road at the bottom of a steep hill. We slowly rolled in and read the sign stating for no trespassers. Most people would up and leave right then. Not us. We were determined to see this place, I mean really see it. I knocked on the door and received no response. I then checked it to see if it was open. As luck would have it, it opened. As I crept in the brightly lit hallway, I noticed all the pictures of Bobby's wins and pictures of Davey, as well. These were pictures that no one had really ever seen before, unless they were to Hueytown. In one of the offices, the light was on. I appeared in the doorway to find a warm-smiling blond haired lady who greeted me with a heartwarming hello. I asked if she didn't mind that I and my family were just looking around, and she opened the door and motioned for them to come on in. What happened next was totally unexpected.

We were talking to Bonnie Allison-Farr, Bobby's daughter! She showed us around inside the building we were in, highlighted by the trophy room, where every single trophy that Bobby, Donnie and Davey ever earned were sitting. I got to try on Bobby's championship jacket, and she let my dad wear Bobby's 1983 Championship ring. It was something just unbelievable. But we weren't done there. Bonnie took us down to the shop, where they were working on a Craftsman Truck to field in 2003, and where one of Bobby's wrecked cars was. It was the one from Pocono- the one he nearly died in. It was off in a dark corner with a tarp over it, and it almost made me break down and cry right there. But, I kept it together, as we moved on to see the old engine dyno which they still use today. It is something quite different than what most dynos look like today, and the big fan contraption at the front of it really added to the old look of it. The final stop was the paint shop, where in it sat an old car driven by Donnie that was being painted for restoration. This was just too much to bear, so we walked back inside where we each received an autograph picture of Bobby Allison, and some leftover championship t-shirts from 1983.

Bonnie also signed the book I had with me. Written by Ed Hinton, it is called Daytona: From the Birth of Speed to the Death of the Man in Black. I highly recommend it to anyone reading this. Amidst many pictures of the shop, and with Bonnie, the time had come to depart. But I will never forget that for a few reasons. First, and most importantly, it was the final vacation I would ever spend with my father, as he tragically passed away this past April. Second, the hospitality shown to us was more than we could ever have asked for. I felt a part of NASCAR history right there. If Bonnie happens upon this story, I want to thank you for your graciousness and for making us feel just a little closer to the sport we love. Until next time, keep those pens flowing and the racin hot, and I will meet you in victory lane!

A One-Race Paint Scheme That Will Never Tell The Whole Story.

By Michael Smith (racefanguide.com)

One-race paint schemes have become a staple at NASCAR events. More often than not, the special paint motif is meant to herald some product or event that a sponsor wants to put in front of the public eye even if the public eye will only see the paint scheme in glimpses snatched at 180 miles per hour. For my money, the best one-race paint schemes are those that speak of times past, or special anniversaries. This season, the Wood Brothers Racing Team is running a series of five different paint schemes to commemorate their 50 years in NASCAR racing. Over the course of five races, the #21 CITGO Ford driven by Elliott Sadler will carry color schemes that replicate cars from the Wood Brothers storied past. At Atlanta Motor Speedway this past March, the CITGO Ford carried the same colors it carried back in 1993 when Morgan Shepherd brought the car across the finish line in first place. Still to come for the CITGO Taurus are four more special paint schemes. At the upcoming 600-mile race at Lowe's Motor Speedway, Elliott Sadler will drive a car bearing the same paint scheme driven by the legendary David Pearson in the 1970s when he clinched 12 straight pole positions and three victories at Charlotte between 1974 and 1979. Then, in July, when NASCAR returns to Daytona, the Wood Brothers car will carry the same colors that Tiny Lund carried on his Wood Brothers Ford Galaxie back in 1963. At Martinsville, the Wood Brothers will commemorate their 50th year in racing with a special paint scheme replicating the convertible that Glen Wood raced back in the 1950s. Finally, on October

15th, the Wood Brothers #21 will roll off the transporter at Talladega wearing the same colors carried by Neil Bonnett when he drove the car to victory in the fall race of 1989.

These one-race paint schemes should really be of interest to NASCAR fans across the nation because they remind us, in a subtle way, where NASCAR has been. The Wood Brothers special paint schemes track the timeline of 50 years worth of hard work, victories won and lost, and storybook finishes. Perhaps the best example is the paint scheme that will be run at Daytona on July 1st. The Wood Brothers will return to Daytona in July with a Ford Taurus that duplicates the paint scheme carried in 1963 when Tiny Lund won the Daytona 500 in storybook fashion. You see Marvin Panch, not Tiny Lund, was the driver for the Wood Brothers when they rolled into Daytona for Speedweeks in 1963. Marvin Panch had some twenty years of racing experience when he joined the Wood Brothers team in 1962. During the '62 season, Panch ran 14 races for Glen and Leonard Wood and, though he didn't post a victory that year, his obvious skills behind the wheel impressed the Wood Brothers because they kept him on for the 1963 season. At the 1963 running of the Daytona 500, Panch qualified the Wood Brothers Galaxie with little fanfare. With several days of Speedweeks still remaining, what else was there to do but drive fast cars? The Briggs Cunningham Masarati team was at Daytona experimenting with Grand National engines and, when they asked Panch if he would take some hot laps in their car, he eagerly accepted. The car did not feel right from the start, and following a stop for fuel and a few adjustments to the car, Panch went back out onto the track. Panch opened the Masarati up, eager to collect a $10,000 prize offered by Bill France to the first driver to break the 180 mile per hour mark, and according to Panch, he almost made the mark when the Masarati went airborne, came down on its side and rolled upside down before coming to a stop near the tunnel turn. Because of the Masarati's design, Panch was trapped in the burning wreckage and the first fire crews on the scene apparently didn't understand his shouted instructions to aim their extinguishers at the burning engine compartment. Their confusion nearly cost Panch his life and would have were it not for a giant of a man called "Tiny" Lund. DeWayne Lund, all 6 feet, 6 inches of him, hailed from Iowa. In a bow to his huge stature, he had been nicknamed "Tiny." In 1963, Lund was at Daytona International Speedway without a steady ride and as the flaming wreckage of Panch's Masarati came to a skidding halt, he was entering the track through the tunnel along with a group of men, including a Firestone Tire engineer. The group of five leapt a fence, ran to the mangled, burning sports car and attempted to lift the car enough to let Panch escape. At the same time, Panch kicked the door out and was halfway free when the fuel tank erupted. Panch's would be-rescuers dropped the car and stepped back, then one shouted that Panch was still trapped and kicking. The men stepped back into the fight and lifted the car again, burning themselves in the process. With the car again lifted, Tiny Lund grabbed Panch by the ankles and dragged him free of the fiery wreckage. Marvin Panch was taken to a nearby hospital where his burns were found to be not life threatening. In a hospital bed conference with Glen and Leonard Wood, it was decided to offer the Wood Brothers ride to Tiny Lund, the man who contributed so much to saving Panch's life. Naturally, being without a ride, Lund accepted. In true storybook fashion, Tiny Lund went on to win the 1963 Daytona 500 in the car he "borrowed" from the Wood Brothers though arguably, through his heroic action, he earned the ride fair and square. The fact that the Daytona 500 marked Lund's first career victory was just more icing on the cake. Add to all this the fact that Lund reportedly ran out of gas as he crossed the finish line and the story has all the makings of a Hollywood thriller. Finally, as if this weren't all just too much, DeWayne Lund would eventually be awarded the Carnegie Medal for Heroism for helping to save Panch's life.

Marvin Panch would recover and continued to drive racecars and win races - for the Wood Brothers Racing Team through the 1966 season. Driving for other teams, Tiny Lund would go on to score four more official NASCAR wins before he lost his life tragically in 1975 while running in the Talladega 500. For those who knew him, and for those who care to keep track of such things, Tiny Lund was truly a giant of a man, both in stature and in heart and soul.

When the green flag drops at Daytona this July 1st, there will be a car on the track that honors not only the 50th anniversary of the Wood Brothers Racing Team, but the bravery of men like Marvin Panch and Tiny Lund and also the fact that, in NASCAR anything is possible. Next Time: The Full Story of the Wood Brothers 50th Anniversary in NASCAR

Addend by Omer Champion. The story you will read below was written my Dave Jr. I have never met him in person but we have been the closest and best friends online for more that 4 years. Dave Jr. is a super nice person and one I am proud to call a friend. I gave Dave Jr. a nickname. He is the only person that I know that can drive a wheelchair 50 miler per hour on his driveway. Maybe that is what inspired me to call him FLASH. YeeHawee to my buddy Dave Jr.

Written by David Peterson, Jr.

My name is David Petersen Jr. but all my racing friends just call me Dave Jr. I'm 39 years old and have been a racing fan for as long as I can remember. I guess you could say my first favorite driver was Speed Racer. In 1974 when I was 10 my dad took me to see the INDY cars race the Rex May Classic in Milwaukee Wisconsin. Seeing real race cars up close got me hooked. As a kid I kept up with racing as much as I could, especially the Indianapolis 500. Growing up in Northern IL. we never really heard much about Stock Car racing except bits and pieces on ABC's Wide World of Sports. Then in 1979 CBS aired the Daytona 500 flag to flag for the first time on tv. I was a die hard INDY car fan but I decided to give this Stock Car racing a chance. From the drop of the green flag I was in awe. I could hardly believe I was actually watching full body stock cars just like you see every day racing the way they did. Seeing these drivers run door to door, beating and banging off of one another completely opened my eyes to a whole new world, the world of NASCAR. As I got older I continued to follow NASCAR becoming more and more a fan with every race I watched. I even had a favorite driver, Dale Earnhardt Sr. When I moved out on my own, I had an apartment just a block away from a sports bar where I met a group of fellow die hard NASCAR fans.

We would meet every Saturday and Sunday to watch the races, each of us cheering on our favorite driver. Watching the races every week became a regular part of my life until Sunday August second 1992. While boating with some friends, I dove into shallow water breaking my neck and injuring my spinal cord. This accident left me permanently paralyzed from the chest down and in a wheel chair for the rest of my life. After five months in the hospital I went home to learn a whole new way of living. I still had NASCAR every weekend, how ever my friends had all moved on and I lost all contact. I went several years without anyone to talk racing with until I discovered the power of the Internet and the strong will of a friend named Dave R P. Dave runs a NASCAR discussion group on the Internet. In that group I met so many interesting racing fans from all around the country. I have become so close to all the friends I have now, I feel like I've known them forever.

Now I have a great life. I have so many great friends, I have a great family and I have NASCAR on the weekends. YEEE HAWEE!

WHAT WAS HE THINKING?

Written by: Elizabeth Wright

The subject: Tony Stewart and his altercation with a photographer.

It's time for me to voice MY opinion, although it may not be popular here goes. One writer is quoted as saying, "Common Courtesy. Professionalism. Lashing out physically at people who are credentialed to stand in the paddock area so they can do their jobs? Unacceptable."

Well you know what, I say it's unacceptable? It's unacceptable for you as a credentialed professional to chase someone one when they are trying to get away from you. The credentials give you the right to take photo's and do interviews but it's a privilege for a reporter to be there not a right and if I had been in a 150 degree car that hot for that long I think I would be ornery too.

Another brilliant quote from a writer and it's a quote verbatim: "What those short-sighted fans don't understand is that without the media, they would not get the exposure to NASCAR stars they currently enjoy. The media is a major reason behind NASCAR's popularity, and should not be subjected to physical violence while trying to do its job."

I agree that no one should be subjected to physical violence but hey, I thought the fans and Drivers made NASCAR what it is, I did not realize that the writers and photographers did! That type of journalist/photographer is the same type of creep that would shove a microphone in someone's face after having lost a loved one and ask "How do you feel." To me THEY are totally unacceptable. Now please remember this number of shock journalist are few in number but they are there. I am not talking about the legitimate ones that work hard to get the information out there to us or share their opinions. As with everything there are good and bad.

Now before y'all go e-mailing me. I do not under ANY circumstances believe that anyone should EVER use physical force on anyone else. I happen to know that some of these journalist plain don't like Tony to begin with and although they say it does not come through in their pieces they are human. They look to push him and that's wrong. I think that NASCAR also needs to look at the photographer and say what were you thinking when you started chasing him, kind of like "AFV" (America's Funniest Video's) when someone does something dumb. What was he thinking? Yes, I see he is running away, o.k., he must want me to chase him and get an action shot. Call it like it is, YES Tony needs anger management and some help, but he also doesn't need people deliberately baiting him. I think now he will be a target to see just how much can we push him. But I don't see NASCAR taking a stand on this and I wish they would. Other less taxing sports get a cool down time, but not NASCAR. It's a draining high adrenaline sport and it's not easy to turn it on or off.

A credential pass gives you the PRIVILEGE of being there not to interfere or run someone down. Now most media and photographers do not behave that way. But just like some fans abuse the privilege of pit passes I believe so do some of the media. Alright, I have said my piece and although it may not be popular it's my opinion and I am out of here running before they photograph me! I would like to send out a YAHOO to Dale Jr. , Michael Waltrip and Steve Park for their great qualifying effort at Michigan!!!!! Way to go guys!!!!

As Always Be Safe and Race Hard!

Elizabeth

FAN DEPRECIATION

NOTE: Please see My STORIES Yeehawee Style for more on the story about the death of Dale Earnhardt and falsely accused Sterling Marlin. I will have to say that this article is very interesting and I can also say that I am in agreement with the context as it is elegantly written by my newfound friend. Here is a big YeeHawee to my new friend. (Omer)

By: Joe Ewert speedwaymedia.com

Sterling Marlin had every right to shove Joel Whitcomb while on vacation. If I were Marlin, I most likely would have done more. But this act of ignorance by the defendant just goes to show what the sport has become, and also what the world has become because of the sport.

Basically, Sterling Marlin was on vacation to relax, have a good time, and enjoy some fun and games during the beach Olympics that were being held. It is not uncommon to see goofing around at others' expense when it comes to friendly competition, such as the display Sterling showed. In the women's tug-of-war match, Sterling stepped in for his team of fans and in joking, pretended to be tugging to help his girls team win.

In my eye, there is nothing wrong with this. It is a friendly game and should be taken in as nothing but fun. Mr. Whitcomb took it one step farther, and treated it as if Marlin knocked him out of the way at Bristol on the last lap. Being an Earnhardt, Jr. fan and having this episode take place in 2001, it is likely that more was said than Marlin being a cheater. He was, after all, the one who received death threats after Dale Earnhardt, Sr.'s death in February of that same year. Knowing NASCAR drivers pretty well, it is a safe assumption to say that Sterling Marlin had had enough of that talk, and showed this guy what was what, and tossed him into two feet of ocean water.

Despite maybe a bruised ego and maybe saltwater in his eyes, I don't see any cause for a swollen knee, and if it was, it surely was not enough to send Mr. Whitcomb into rehab for months before it healed. I am not a medical expert, but it does not take a rocket scientist to see that these injuries were possibly over exaggerated because it was a millionaire NASCAR driver and not Joe Schmo from Kokomo. If it were Mr. Schmo and not Sterling Marlin, the situation would have been different and a lawsuit would not be likely.

These kinds of incidents are putting a black cloud over the sport we love so much. It s getting to the point where the drivers can't even be human anymore. Sterling acted as a human being, and not a puppet for sponsors who goes on television and says how good the car is and thanks Coors and Dodge and whoever else is plastered on the side of that car. I have had conversations with drivers whom I will not mention named, but they have said names of drivers, situations, etc., that they really liked or really disliked. However, they said they cannot express these feelings due to their image they must maintain. To me, this is sad. It is the fans, this time, who should be scolded. Not the true blue, all the way, fully blown NASCAR fans, but the so-called "newbies". The people who watch just for the wrecks, or cheer Jeff Gordon because they like Pepsi, ought to be reprimanded for their behavior towards the drivers. It has come to the point where they have to put on their face all the time, even when they have family time or just want to collect their thoughts. These new fans have taken advantage of the fact that NASCAR drivers are the most accessible athletes in sports, they have taken advantage of their favorite driver's kindness on camera, as well. When they come face to face with them, they expect the same kind smile and everything that goes along with it, but that is not always the case. It is to the point that a rude look on a driver's face or refusing to sign an autograph lands the driver in hot water for failing to meet their obligations as an ambassador to the sport, and to me, that is unfair. Until next time, keep those pens flowing and the racing hot, and I just might meet you in victory lane.

speedwaymedia.com

THE MAN IN BLACK

NOTE: Joe Ewert is one of my new found friends. As I usually do when I meet a new friend, I give them a nickname. Please meet my new friend, ACE. (Omer)

Written by: Joe Ewert

My family was always a mix of Earnhardt fans, and non-Earnhardt fans. My father and uncle both worked for General Motors, and my other uncle worked for MAC Tools, which was always a sponsor Dale had on his car. Ever since I was born, it has been Dale, Dale, and Dale. I dreamed of what it would be like to one day meet this glorified man. Finally, I got my chance.

The year was 1990, and I had just turned six years old, but this day I can remember as if it were yesterday. My aunt told me Dale Earnhardt was at a local Chevy dealer, and she was taking me to meet him. Excitement filled my body as she loaded me up in her red 1984 Camaro and in the blink of an eye, we were there. As we stood in line, I just could not believe that Dale was a few feet away and all these people were in my way. So, being the gracious little boy I am, I kindly asked grown adults to move out of my way because "my friend Dale Earnhardt wants to meet me". They just smiled and maintained their spot in line, and I was quickly hushed.

My aunt then told me to just wait my turn, and then let me in line by myself. Another form of exhilaration filled my pint-sized body as I knew I was going to have to say something to him, but I had no idea what. It was at that moment that I overheard Dale ask a PR person to get him something to eat because he was starvin'. Right then, I thought that having him at my house for dinner was not such a bad idea, after all, my grandma was cooking a stew and there were always plenty of leftovers.

It was about time. My turn to meet the man I had heard so much about and had seen on TV and everything else. In my double small Goodwrench t-shirt, I approached him timidly. I was greeted with a warm smile as Dale asked "What's your name, good buddy?"

"J-J-Joey, and I think you are great," was all I could muster. In the mind of a six year old, that was pretty darn cool to say.

"You do? Well hey that's just great. And you know what I do to people who think I am great? I shake their hand. Put her there, Joey." Dale boasted, as if it was his own son he was talking to. He shook my hand, careful not to squeeze too tight, and then handed me an autographed card with him and the previous year's Winston Cup trophy. I couldn't let him give me something without me giving him something in return, so I asked for his marker. He hesitated for a second, and then gave it to me in an "oh-what-the-heck" manner. I yanked a bent up soccer card of myself from the Rec. Department soccer team I was on, roughly signed "To 3, Joey". Upon handing him the card, I asked if he'd like to have dinner with us, because my grandma was making stew and it was my favorite.

Most professional athletes are snobs. They sign their autographs, and then brush away fans, including kids who look up to them as gods. What I love about NASCAR are experiences like this one. He gave me a million-dollar smile and said it was his favorite, too, but he had to catch a plane to Michigan for the next race, but he would put the card in the car with him during the race. Whether he did or not I will never know, but knowing "The Intimidator", I'd say that he did, in fact, do just that. Until next time, keep the pens flowing and the racing safe, and I'll see you in victory lane.

A MILLION SEATS AT BRISTOL

Written by: J. C. Hodges

When I was about 25 years old I went to my first race at Bristol, that was before it had a million seats like it does now. Just kidding. I had seen a whole lot of races on television, but what a thrill it was to see my first race in person. I never was a good writer, but I hope it will be good enough for Omer to put in his book. I won't be able to tell it good enough to even come close to letting you know what a great time and a thrilling day I had.

It was almost unbelievable to see the car running that fast on such a small track. Of all the beating, banging and wrecking I have ever seen it sure took place that day. On television while I was watching just didn't make the same impression as it did live and in person. About every 10 or 15 lap it was a caution and I can remember my friend Alex keeping count of them. On that day there were 19 cautions and I think the record was broken in 2003 and is now 20. Anyway, it was a thriller. I wish I could write better, but I just can't seem to tell how great it was. The race was won by Darrell Waltrip and he had won several races at that track and now holds the track record for the most wins. My favorite driver was Cale Yarborough and he was the one who called Darrell Jaws. When the race was over me and Alex decided to hang around to let the crowd clear up. We wanted to just walk around and take a look at everything and maybe check out the souvenir trailers. We had a ball and it was cool to see everything they had to sell. I bought me a Cale Yarborough shirt and Alex bought a Richard Petty shirt. I wanted to wear my shirt and didn't want to wait until I got home to do it. I had a back pack on. I took my old shirt off and put it in my back pace and then put on my new Cale Yarborough shirt. I was one proud fool to be in my new shirt. By this time the race had been over for about 4 hours and most of the fans had cleared out. We started leaving the speedway and just before we got to the bridge, we was a group of people just standing around like they were waiting for something. I soon found out that they were near a van owned by Darrell Waltrip and was waiting for him to come to drive it home or back to his motel. Because Darrell had won the race he had to stay inside to take pictures, go to the press box and do some promotion for his sponsor Gatorade. That is why so many people was standing around. They knew that he was still inside the track. We stood there for about 30 minutes and I could see Darrell and his wife who's name was Stevie. They were walking down the hill and when he got to the group of people he stopped and started signing autographs. So many people were in front of me that I didn't know if I would be able to get his autograph before he left. Stevie was standing there just waiting for him to finish and I thought I would go talk to her. She was so nice and seemed like a Christian person or at least someone that love everyone. When we started talking she noticed my new Cale shirt. I told her I wished I had a Darrell shirt and I could get him to sign it for me. She said, Darrell don't care, he will sign that shirt. That made me excited and I sure was hoping he would not leave before I got to him. About that time Stevie got Darrell's attention and told him I wanted him to sign my Cale shirt. Stevie then started laughing and then Darrell said come over here. I walked over to him and he was so nice and said You like Cale, do you? He said, that is alright, I like him too. He said turn around and I will sign it on the back. He signed the back of my shirt and I could not see it. Alex told me to take the shirt off and look at the autograph that Darrell signed. On the back of the shirt, he drew a little picture of a shark and signed it Jaws. From that day on I was a Darrell Waltrip fan and Cale was my second favorite. I rooted for Darrell until he retired.

FROM THE CRIB TO THE TRACK

Written by: Jenny (MoParJenny)

I never really have gone to an actual NASCAR race, but I have attended many local tracks here in Virginia. Raceways such as Southside Speedway, where Lennie Pond began his racing career, and Virginia Motor Speedway, which is where many sprint car drivers have came for side-by-side dirt oval racing action.

Ever since I was about five years old, I have gone to the closest race track to my house - Southside Speedway. In fact, it is so close to my crib, that on Friday nights, you can hear to announcer on the intercom! I remember one certain Friday night during the local track racing season a few years back to when I was about seven years of age. My father and I went to Southside Speedway for their annual Old-Timers Night. It's a night when surviving racers that crossed the finish line decades ago show up to show-off their ancient race cars and take a few laps around the track. My dad had bought me a checkered flag from one of the souvenir stands before the actual racing started. Most of the weekly races were really exciting, except for maybe a couple. When the main event was about to start, it was finally time to pull out the cameras. The gorgeous, full restored stock cars from the past made their way onto the 3/8 mile paved track. After the annual event took place, some spectators went to their cars to head home, while others headed straight for the pit area - that included me and my father. We went around, talking to various racers, me getting their autographs on my checkered flag.

When we were almost finished, and about to leave for home, we just had to spark a conversation based on old memories about the sport's past with a certain veteran - Lennie Pond. He signed the flag right in the middle white square! It was just one of those moments that not many people are able to experience during their lifetime. That particular checkered flag that was purchased for only ten dollars, is now hanging in its own special place on a wall in my bedroom. It probably is worth a thousand words.

KENTUCKY BOYS TO THE RESCUE

Written by: Carl Robinson

I was so happy when I heard that the YeeHawee Man was going to write a book and let his friends write something in the book about racing. When I heard about this, I was so excited to hear about his book. I know one thing for sure which I would like to tell everyone who reads his book. What I would like to tell you is about meeting the YeeHawee man and all of those nice folks that came to Atlanta on a chartered bus. I can't remember what the name of the YeeHawee man was, but I do remember the driver of the bus had a funny name like Hootie or Shootie. Do you remember the winter that we had that snow storm in Atlanta and the race was almost postponed? I am glad that they had the race, even if I did almost freeze to death. The temperature at the race track on race day was down in the twenties and that sure is cold for Atlanta. Well, anyway, I still went to the race and on that day, I met some of the nicest race fans that you would ever find. There were about 30 or 40 people on the bus. When I saw the bus, it was just sitting there with the engine running and I guess everyone was trying to get warm after sitting in the cold grandstand all day. I had tried to jump a small branch that day which was covered over with ice, but I slipped and fell through the ice. It was only about 6 inches deep, but I still got soaking wet. I was so cold that I was shivering. I went by the bus and knocked on the door and the driver opened the door and asked me what I wanted. I told him I wanted to just come inside and warm up for a little while. He sure was a nice man and he was always laughing about something, He told me I was welcome to come in and warm up, but I had better not get out of line because the bouncer will throw you off of the bus. I sure didn't want a big brute bouncer to throw me off the bus. When he showed me the bouncer, I like to died in my shoes. That bouncer was not bigger than a Georgia F__T, but he turned out to be nicest and one of the friendliest men I have ever met. There was a man on the bus that was the football coach at the high school in Kentucky. He sure was a talker, but everyone liked him. I can also remember a man that was a used car dealer in Kentucky. I can remember a great big guy that I thought should be the bouncer and I found out that he was kin to the football coach. Oh yes, I can remember that there was even a doctor on the bus. He worked at a Kentucky hospital and was a Syke doctor. The coach said they everyone else was his patients. He was just kidding. That was funny. I sure wish I knew some of those names, but I can't remember any of them, but I will never forget what a great time we had on the bus. The driver even bought food for everyone and he let me eat with them. OH, one more thing. There was a young man on the bus that bless his heart he was a deaf mute and I found out the the driver let him go on the trip free and even bought him a 70 dollar ticket to the race. Things like this is why I wanted to write my little story. That just goes to show you what a great bunch of nice people you can meet for Kentucky.

I guess I have talked enough, but I hope that the YeeHawee man's friends all buy his book so that you will know that I appreciate you being so kind to me when I was so cold and almost frozen to death.

MY LIFE AND RACING

Written by: Mike (aka Spanky from MO)

I have been a racing fan for as long as I can remember. This is due to the fact that my dad started taking me to the local stock car races when I was only two years old. I don't remember those early trips but I do know now that I fell in love with the sights, sounds and smells of racing at a very early age. My dad began going to races in 1948 and went to his first Nascar Grand National race in 1955, when I was just one year old. Living in Southeast Missouri we didn't have many chances to see Nascar racing but this race was held in Lehi, Arkansas at the Memphis-Arkansas Speedway. He got to see Tim and Fonty Flock, Lee Petty, Buck Baker and all the other big names of the time. As time went on I became more and more interested in racing and kept up with Nascar by looking through the pages of Hot Rod magazine, which would occasionally have an article about one of the big races, and looking through the sports section of the Memphis, TN newspaper. I still have a copy of the issue of Hot Rod telling about the building of Daytona Speedway. By 1960 I knew enough about Nascar racing to have a racing idol and it was none other than Glenn "Fireball" Roberts. I scoured the results of every race to see where Fireball had finished. While all the other kids at school idolized Stan Musial, Roger Maris and

Mickey Mantle I had Fireball and Little Joe Weatherly. Finally in 1962 my dad was going to another Nascar race and not just any race. He was going to the Daytona 500. I wasn't very happy because I couldn't make the trip and I could hardly wait for him to get back so I could hear every detail about the race. I was overjoyed to hear that Fireball had won the race. Daddy said the gold top of Fireball's car shone so bright you could spot it anywhere on the track. It almost broke my heart when Fireball switched to Fords in 1963 but he was still my racing hero. Then came 1964. At the very start of the year Nascar lost their champion in an accident at Riverside. Little Joe was gone. Then came Charlotte and Fireball was critically burned in an accident. In just a few short weeks my hero was gone also.

Finally in 1966 I got to go to my first Nascar race. The whole family was going to Nashville and I would finally get to see all my idols race. I was especially looking forward to seeing this guy I had been reading about and seeing in ads in the back of Hot Rod, a fellow by the name of Bobby Allison. Bobby led a lot of the race in his little Chevelle but blew his engine. Little did he know it but he had gained a fan that night for as long as he continued to drive. Since that night in 1966 I've been to many races at several race tracks including the infamous first race held at Talladega in 1969. The last Nascar race I attended was the 1995 Daytona 500 and I got to see my favorite modern day driver, Sterling Marlin, win his second Daytona 500 in a row. Even better than that I got to see Bobby Allison again and get some autographs from him. This was one of the best racing trips I ever took.

I guess I'll be a Nascar fan until the day that I die even if they do keep trying to let the people with money ruin it.

"MY ONLINE RACING BUDDIES"

Written by: Maggie Hawes

How I met my good friend Omer and all my other race fan friends; but how do I begin? I guess at the very beginning would be the best place. Several years ago, I use to visit a webtv race discussion group called 'thisisn'tmynic'. We started having trouble makers disrupting the group and I stopped going there. In the meantime, the "owner" of the group must have left too, because when I dropped in for a visit several months later, there were only a few posters, mainly Dave RP, and at first, I thought he was talking to himself. The troublemaker's were gone, so I decided to hang around for awhile........... that was at least three years ago and I'm still hangin'. {smile}During that time, Omer & other's started posting and our little group began to grow. We are now a group of caring friends who share our love of racing, as well as have a "YEEE HAWEEEIN" good time. Omer has nicknames for almost everyone in the group; Dave RP kept the group going after many of us left and is our leader or as Omer has named him..... "Daddy", he keeps us all in line....... or at least tries. I'm Maggie, also known as "Mommy", because I think I'm the only female that's been with the group since the beginning; also have the nic "Flower Child", because of my love of flowers. Our Omer & his lovely wife Jo are more then cyber-friends, they are our _real_ friends and both mean a great deal to all of us. Many have been lucky enough to meet them in person, I hope one day I'll be one of the "lucky ones".

Omer Dear Friend, I wish only the best for you and your family; you are a very special person, one I'm proud to call my "Buddy".

Written by: Jan Jensen

I first began watching NASCAR on that fateful day of February 18, 2001, at the urging of a former boyfriend who, was himself, very much a NASCAR fan. At first I was rather bored with watching what appeared to me as toy cars going around and around on a track called "Daytona", but just as I was about to switch television stations, Tony Stewart's #20 Home Depot car began it's lift off and started flipping over and over sending a tremendous chill through my spine. Fearing Stewart dead, I shut off my TV. I swore off NASCAR from that moment not wanting to partake in the viewing of a sport where crashing and dying were all "just part of the game". My boyfriend called a few minutes later and told me Stewart was ok and explained how well those race cars protected the drivers with braces and roll bars and such and that incidents like Stewart's "rarely happened". Under protest, I turned the race back on and continued watching, flinching every time a car so closely passed by another but then began to take great interest in the strategy these drivers displayed. I wondered how if everyone was going the approximate same speed, could one pass another and how others could be laps down. I began to root for the #3 car, watching his moves and thinking "Wow, this guy is good!". He was doing a move I kept hearing the commentators call as the "Bump and Run". I had no idea he was, Mr. Dale Earnhardt Sr., "The Intimidator", the "Big E", the gentleman of whom I had heard my boyfriend boast so much about. The same wonderful man whom I had met at a charity function several years earlier and replied to him that I had never even heard of "stock car racing" when questioned if I was a fan. As the race neared the finish, I felt quite positive Mr. Earnhardt would win, when suddenly I witnessed his car swerve into the wall and crash head on. I had witnessed many car accident scenes in the past while working with paramedics, the crash did not appear to me to be a cause for significant injury, let alone a death and being the race was now over, I went about my day not giving it a second thought. It was of great shock to later get a phone call from my boyfriend telling me that Mr. Dale Earnhardt Sr. had succumbed to the injuries inflicted in his crash. I again stated my plan to my boyfriend of never watching this so called sport of "stock car racing" again when he pointed out that Mr. Earnhardt also had a son racing that day, in the very same race! He asked if I thought this son would give up the sport too after having witnessed the same accident. I believed Dale Earnhardt Jr's opinion would not be much different than mine as this was his father and now he is gone. We then spoke in detail of fathers and sons who had raced in the past and of those who have lost fathers and sons to the sport. I agreed to watch a second race the following week. I watched how the fans reacted after the death of one of their most beloved icons, I watched how the drivers reacted, and I saw Dale Jr. there in the line up as well. I thought if he could brave it out, then so could I. It was then that I looked more at who was behind those steering wheels than at what color the pretty car was or who manufactured it. I started reading bio's on NASCAR.com and watching their behavior both on and off the track. I learned that Tony Stewart turned 7 the day my son was born and that Jeff Gordon and Kevin Harvick were from my own home state of California. I learned several of the drivers had interest in different charities and made appearances and sponsored drives for them. I learned many have beautiful families who must deal with their prolonged absences while the season is on. I also learned that while some drivers had their own sorrow to deal with, without much time off to regroup themselves, they persevered.

I appreciate NASCAR's convictions of penalty for foul behavior and that for the most part, the drivers adhere to the rules and refrain from lifestyles that would target them for "bad press". I pray every day Steve Park and Jerry Nadeau overcome their injuries and return fully to the circuit as they hope to. Becoming ill myself with an incurable muscle disorder, I have learned through these two men that willpower and want is much stronger a "drug" than any medicine a doctor could prescribe me.

Dale Jarrett, who will always be my most favorite driver, and Bill Elliott have taught me that no matter how bad the situation is, to smile anyway and remain positive, there is always a "next time". Many of these NASCAR drivers hold special places in my heart and not only because they can skillfully drive real fast in their colorfully painted cars every week for my entertainment, but also because of who they are personally and what they do to give back to their communities because of who they are. I thank them for "being there" for me and their families for "lending" them to me, each week. (I'd give anything to meet Mr. Dale Jarrett) I also thank my former boyfriend for turning me on to the sport of NASCAR. My home is filled with memorabilia and my head spins with the memories of great races gone by. My life, without a doubt, is so much more enriched because of NASCAR and I am in turn forever it's fan. - Jan Jensen

I MET FIREBALL ROBERTS ONE DAY

By: Raymond Belcher

I guess I am older than most of the race fans today because I am even older than Fireball Roberts. The reason I mentioned Fireball was because he was my favorite driver back during the beach racing days. I have never been to a race on the big speedways, but I sure saw my share of the beach and dirt track races. Curtis Turner was the best on dirt, but Fireball was the best at the beach. I don't know Omer, but I saw a story he wrote that told us about his first driver being Fireball Roberts. I wanted to tell him about me meeting Fireball one day and I will always remember that.

I went to a beach race in 1957. I always put up a little tarp up on a small knoll that made me high enough to get a good view of the race. About half way through the race, Fireball blew his engine real close to where I was sitting. He got out of the car and walked up to where I was and sit down in one of my chairs under the tarp. He asked me for a cigarette. I gave him a Chesterfield. He thanked me and said that he was a Luck Strike smoker, but he would take what I had. We talked, smoked and drank a coke for about 20 minutes and then he left. I had really met what I call a man. They don't make like that anymore. He would destroy the drivers that we have now. I can't type, but my grandson Charles, typed this as I told him what I wanted to say. Charles goes to the races today and I would like to go with him, but I am not well enough to go. I hope you liked my story.

Raymond

ROGER, GLENN, SARGE and OMER

Written by: Roger from Georgia

I told Omer I would like to write something about him and I wanted him to put it in his new book that he is writing. I don't even know if he has finished it the book or not, but I know it will be a great book if he writes it. I guess I should have told everyone who I was at the beginning, but I am not very good at writing things. My name is not important, but Omer and my buddies know me as Roger from Georgia. I have been a race fan since 1990, and I go to about 3 races each year, but I have never missed being at Talladega since 1990. I met Omer about 5 years ago at Talladega.

I went to Talladega with one my friends named Glenn. When we got there and set up camp we were camping next to an older gentleman from Florida that everyone called Sarge. Sarge had been a race fan for about 30 years and he seemed to know everything about the races. I told Sarge that I sure was amazed at how much he seemed to know about Nascar Racing. Sarge said you haven't seen nothing yet, just wait until tomorrow and I will introduce you to a man named Omer that everyone calls HeHaw. He told me he would bet me 50 dollars that Omer could answer more questions about Nascar than any 5 people he could find in the campground. He meant counting all 5 of the people's score as one he pitted against. I told Sarge that I didn't want to bet 50 dollars, but I would take 10 dollars of it. Sarge said it was a deal and he would go get Omer tomorrow when he comes. Sarge talked a lot about Omer and told me his son was going to be a pilot in the air force. Sarge sure did know a lot about Omer and I was looking forward to meeting this guy that knew so much. The next day I was trying to put up a new canopy Glenn and I had bought before we got to Talladega. The damn thing was almost driving us crazy trying to put it up. The wind was blowing and we never had a canopy before and had no idea how to put it up. While Glenn and I were working trying to get the canopy up, I looked up and saw a little old man walking toward us. When he got there he told us he would like to help us put up the canopy because he had one just like ours and it would be easy for him to put it up. While we were working together, we were all talking and got to know each other pretty well, but we still didn't know this man's name that was helping us. We got the canopy put up and thanked the man for helping us and asked him his name. He said My name is Omer and I am from Kentucky. Well I almost S-- in my pants. I had just met Omer before Sarge could introduce him to me. Sarge had gone to the International Motorsports Hall of Fame and should be back soon. I started talking to Omer and told him everything Sarge had said about him. I also told Omer about the bet I had made with Sarge. Omer started laughing and said he and Sarge were good friends and he would like to pull a joke on Sarge that would backfire in his face. Omer kept smiling and said for me to make another bet with Sarge and he would miss all of the answers so that I could win. He also said after it was over we would tell Sarge the truth and give Sarge his money back. I just knew that knowing Omer was going to be lots of fun. About 2 hours later I saw Sarge walking to the campsite. Omer was at his van. When Sarge got there the first thing he said was I saw Omer over there and I am going to go get him for you and Glenn to meet. While Sarge went to get Omer, Glenn and I liked to laugh our self to death. We just knew we were going to have a ball. Here came Sarge with Omer and it was all we could do to keep from laughing. We talked about 15 minutes, then I bet Sarge 20 dollars that Omer could not answer 5 questions out of 10 questions. Boy, you should have seen how fast Sarge started getting the money out of his billfold. Glenn made up the 10 questions and Sarge read them off to Omer. Omer started missing every question until he got to question number 4. I then asked Sarge if he wanted to call off the bet and he said yes. Omer, Glenn and me all started laughing at the same time and Sarge realized that he had been framed.

We all started high five-ing each other and Sarge liked to killed Omer with his big bear hug. We also agreed to call off the 10 dollar bet. Glenn and I still wanted to put Omer to the test, but all for fun with no bets. Sarge made up 10 questions and Omer answered all 10 of them and even told us additional information about the last question number 10. The no. 10 question was about Mark Martin. I will never forget this and I think of it very often. When Omer answered the question about Mark, he also said did you know his wife was named Arleen and he has a son named Matt that drives go cart races. That liked to blowed my mind. That is the end of my story about Omer. I can say in all honesty, Omer was and still is my favorite racing fan. We have been camping together for about 5 years and it is always a pleasure to see him coming with his trademark HeHaw shout. Guess, I will be signing off.

Yours Truly,
Roger

POEMS YEEHAWEE STYLE

Written by: Rachel Nichols

~I'm A NASCAR Fan~

Don't give me diamonds
they aren't my friend,
gimmie the Fox Crew
and my MRN.
Richmond and Bristol
racing under the lights,
rush hour with intense speeds
hey, it's just what I like.
I'm A NASCAR fan !!
The smell of burning rubber
is such a sweet thing,
fourteen second pit stops
makes my heart sing.
From turn three at Daytona
to the wrenches turning in the garage,
getting your team in the lead
this isn't no mirage.
Fans cheering for their driver
buying their die cast cars,
keeping your eyes open
on the fastest new superstars.
I'm a NASCAR Fan !!!
Heading to the track..
for a three day weekend,
meeting old and new friends
while making memories that will never end.
Sitting back to reminisce
of the good ol' days,
from who was the toughest

202

to the one with the intimidating ways.
I'm A NASCAR Fan !!!
From Watkins Glen in New York
across to California Speedway,
fans know the day of rest
is a day for hard play.
Four or five hundred miles
us fans don't really care,
where ever there is a race
us fans will be there!!
I'm A NASCAR Fan!

By Cynthia Guenthner

a/k/a "Frozen Tundra"

`Twas the night before Christmas and at the North Pole
Already the winter had taken its toll.
The barn door flew open from the strong, chilly breeze
And in stumbled Rudolph; he started to sneeze.
The light had completely gone out of his nose; He shook
and he trembled from his head to his toes.
Mrs. Santa remarked, "Why Rudolph, you look quite a
fright
There's no way you can lead Santa's sleigh tonight!"
Santa sighed and sobbed, "Dear, what will I do? It's
Rudolph's big night, but he's got the flu!"
She kindly reminded him, "When you're in a bad way,
Ask God for an answer-Santa, just pray."
"Lord, my trustiest reindeer's come down with a cold. I
can't do it alone, for I'm getting too old!"
Then God came to Santa in a brilliant white light
Assuring him He would provide for that night.
"We've got a new angel; he came just this year. He's
faster, much faster than any reindeer.

You'll know when his shiny black car you will see
It's faster than lightning with a big number "3."
Before he could even get up off his knee
Santa looked up to behold the Black Number 3.
But suddenly the grandfather clock struck midnight.
Santa said, "I give up-there's no time to make the whole flight."
The driver calmly said, "Just load up the toys. We'll make sure there's Christmas for all girls and boys."
When they finished loading, he said, "Hop right inside. We're going to make a record-time ride.
"But meanwhile at NOAA, the trackers were worried.
"We haven't spotted Santa; we sure hope he hurries!"
When a quarter past midnight a small blip appears.
"Why it must be Santa, but that's no reindeer!
"By 3:45 their journey complete, Santa exclaimed, "I can't believe we've accomplished this feat!
All gifts were delivered in time record breaking
So quickly and easily, and I'm not even aching!"
Back at the North Pole was the red-nosed reindeer
Standing in awe and shedding a tear.
Saying, "Santa, I see that you need me no more.
Well, I'll have to retire; just show me the door."
"Wait a minute, Rudolph," said the driver of "3,"
"I'll teach you to fly, maybe faster than me."
So if some starry night you see a flash in the heavens
It might be the Black 3's giving Rudolph flying lessons.
And then by next Christmas, quite a sight you will see,
Merry Christmas from Santa, Rudolph, and the Black Number "3"

THE MAN

By Richard H. Monroe

He was just a normal southern guy,
A plain and simple gent.
He grew up with a racing Dad,
And to the tracks they went.
Times were not the best for them,
They had bad days and good.
But his favorite times were in the shop,
With his Dad, under the hood.
It really came as no surprise
though Ralph did not agree,
When Dale left school, to go and race,
And follow his own dream.
Then one day, Dale's world was crushed,
When he went to help his Dad.
And found him laying by the car,
He knew then, he was dead.
But with love of racing in his blood,
And a fire from deep within.
Dale set out to make Ralph proud,
His only goal, to win.
It seemed his Dad was watching him,
And guiding from above.
As he circled home tracks every week,
Up The Ranks of the sport he loved.
It took some time to get there,
But to the top, he went.
Top rookie honors, his first year,
The next, he was the champ.
No other driver ever,
Has duplicated this feat.
It seemed, he was to be the best,

To ever grace that seat.
Thru the years, he made it to the top
Six more times after that.
A feat that tied the record set,
By a King in a cowboy hat.
Dale also raced in IROC,
With others, all the best.
And four times won the championship,
He was passing every test.
It took him twenty years,
To win NASCAR's Super Bowl.
To prove the critics wrong, when they said,
His age was taking it's toll.
Then on February eighteenth,
In the year two thousand one.
They dropped the green flag one more time,
The season had begun.
It seemed that this would be Dales year,
To take home number eight.
And might have occurred, had it not been, For the
intervention of fate.
In two of his cars, Michael leads,
With Jr. close behind.
And then was Dale, running third,
Protecting them on his mind.
In the last turn, of the last lap,
His car went to the wall.
And as we all watched Michael win,
Dale answered Heaven's call.
There's really not much more to say,
You can't question our Maker's plan
But for these reasons, and many more,
Dale will always be "THE MAN"

THE INTIMIDATOR

By Jenny

You were the King of racing, even as the years went by, you didn't know how big you were, but in our hearts you were flying high. You were Dale Earnhardt, the Intimidator, the best of the best, it is with great grief and mourning, that you have to be laid to rest. You had always seemed invincible, we never thought you would stop, we always new number three, would be patrolling the track like a cop. When you finally won Daytona, we were celebrating all the more, when your unicorn struck back upon you, our hearts hit the floor. You were almost a god, definitely enshrined in racing immortality, now thanks to turn four, you are a racing fatality. We worshiped the ground you walked on, you were a hero
to all, we never in our wildest dreams, could conceive that our hero would fall. We love you Dale, you will be missed greatly.

Chasin A Rainbow

By Trish
(http://members.aol/.com/winstongal/nascarlinks.htm)

In fairy tales a story is told
Of a colorful rainbow and a pot of gold
We've all seen rainbows after a long rain
But there's a special kind of rainbow with its own name
This rainbow rides on Goodyears and has horses under the hood
A crew chief and a pit crew that's certainly very good
An appetite that's hungry and always wants more
And a big 24 on both of its doors

But something makes this rainbow one of a kind
A driver that races with his heart and his mind
He's young, ambitious and has a racing desire
He rushes through the pack like a burning fire
So next time you decide to chase a rainbow,you better watch you step.. 'Cause it could be the rainbow, everyone calls&JEFF.

"Racing The Wind"

FOR Ray Evernham

With his crew chief and pit crew behind him all the way
Jeff Gordon races the best he can, come Race Sunday The qualifying laps and practice session
Are equally important in his racing profession
But the most unique quality that he has
Is winning races and running them fast
He races with courage and a competitive attitude
And whether he's being cheered or being booed
He holds his head high until the very end
And he gets out there and races like he was racing the wind
Warrior Spirit Winning is in his blood and victory is in his heart
His heartbeat is the thunder that his driver thrives on
The fire in his soul is the lightning that feeds the storm
And the gleam in his eye is the flame that leads the way
He's the man behind the man who makes his way to victory lane
He watches over Jeff Gordon every lap around the track
And talks him through every turn and to the checkered flag
Ray Evernham has become a fighter all his own

And will continue to be the crew chief with the winning warrior spirit

The Warrior Inside He comes through the turns like the speed of light

One blink of the eye and he's gone, clear out of sight Back around he comes faster than before

He flies right by, you can hardly see the 24 on his door What makes him so determined and so full of pride? What else could it be but Jeff Gordon and the warrior inside?

Never Will They Fall As a team they work together as teams are supposed to do

The triumphs they make together are far more than few

They tend to the every needs of the #24 Dupont ride Whether in the garage or running in the turns three or four wide

The team that works together wins together and this team does it all

For more years to come, they'll continue to rise and never will they fall.

Dedicated To The "Rainbow Warriors"

My OPINIONS YeeHawee Style

10 GREATEST DRIVERS OF ALL TIMES

THE 10 GREATEST DRIVERS OF ALL TIMES

When the above mentioned topic comes up for discussion, we could probably have thousands of different opinions. Why? Because there are no exact ways of determining who are the greatest drivers of all times. Times, cars, tracks, drivers, technology and others things have changed so drastically that we can not compare a driver who drove in different era's of racing. Just because a driver won 40 races, doesn't necessarily mean he was a better driver than a driver that won 10 races. The 40 win driver may have had a better car, better equipment and more money to work with. The 10 win driver could have been less fortunate, but could be a better driver.

Now, I think we all playing on a level field. According to what I have just written, we can not pick the greatest drivers of all time. However, we do have our on feelings and I will try to express my feeling for this topic. I will endeavor to pick the 10 greatest drivers of all times, but I would like to just mention some of the greatest drivers just to refresh your memory. In the beginning of the sport when it was organized in 1948 some of the top drivers were: Lee Petty, Tim Flock, Fonty Flock, Curtis Turner, Little Joe Weatherly, Herb Thomas, Junior Johnson, Fireball Roberts, Cotton Owens, Buck Baker, Red Byron, Ned Jarrett Rex White and many others.

When we move on into the middle of the time period for the 60's and 70's era we find lots more great drivers such as: Richard Petty, David Pearson, Cale Yarborough, Bobby Allison, Buddy Baker, Fred Lorenzen, Bobby Isaac, Tiny Lund, Darrell Waltrip, Neil Bonnett, Donnie Allison and others.

Later on in the last 30 years we have had, Dale Earnhardt, Rusty Wallace, Mark Martin, Terry Labonte, Ricky Rudd, Bobby Labonte, Tim Richmond, Davey Allison, Bill Elliott and many more great drivers.

This brings us to today, where we have so many young guns that have come into racing to make a mark on the sport. Some of those drivers are Jeff Gordon, Tony Stewart, Jeff Burton, Kurt Busch, Jeremy Mayfield, Ryan Newman, Dale Earnhardt, Jr., Jamie McMurray, Johnny Benson, Kevin Harvick, Robby Gordon and many more.

Now that I have helped you remember some of the greatest drivers in our sport, I will try to the best of my knowledge and based on my 46 years of experience, to pick my 10 greatest drivers of all times.

1 Richard Petty
2 David Pearson
3 Fireball Roberts
4 Cale Yarborough
5 Bobby Allison
6 Dale Earnhardt
7 Darrell Waltrip
8 Jeff Gordon
9 Fred Lorenzen
10 Junior Johnson

NOTE; A. J. Foyt was not considered in my 10 choices, because he was not a full time driver in Nascar. Had A. J. been a full time driver, I am sure he would have made the list. I will leave it here, but saying that A. J. Foyt was one of the greatest drivers in the world. YeeHawee to A.J.

WE ALL LOVE IT IN DIFFERENT WAYS

Isn't is amazing how we all love this great sport of ours, but we can sure see things from many different prospectives. I guess that is why we have so many different hats at the race track. Some of us love a certain driver and at the same time others absolutely hate him. Jeff Gordon and Dale Earnhardt were two very controversial drivers that the fan either loved or hated. However, I am not they type of fan that would ever hate any driver regardless of who he may be. Never in my life would you ever hear me say that I hope a driver hits the wall that causes injury or even death. I do have my favorites in the best sport on Earth, but I can honestly say that I like and respect all drivers. It takes all types of driver to make up the sport as it takes all kind of fans like us to help keep the excitement and interest going. When you are at the race and start looking at the hats and shirts that the fans wear, it wouldn't take long to see that Jeff Gordon and Dale Earnhardt (when he was with us) probably have more fans than the combined total of all of the other drivers. If you are/or were a fan of Dale or Jeff, you would almost love them. Some fans go so far as to get tattoos of them on their body.

Some fans even paint their house in their colors. It is a very amazing thing to be this dedicated to a driver and it is almost like worshiping the. Well now, how do I know this? I have been there and have been a fan of Richard Petty ever since my first favorite driver Fireball Roberts left us in that blazing flame at Charlotte in 1964. I have been a Richard Petty fan for almost 40 years and believe it or not my family have accused me of worshiping him. However, God is the number one person in my life and I don't worship Richard, but I do think he is the greatest race driver that ever lived. I also think he is a humanitarian, leader, gentlemen and a great role model for us to follow. I guess you can see that I am already excited by just talking about him. I have met and talked to him more than a hundred times and every time I meet him, he make me feel more important that he really is. The man is very special and if you ever meet and talk to him, I will guarantee that you will feel like you did him a favor by talking to him. OH well, I guess I have been babbling about Richard so much that I have overlooked the main subject of what I had intended to write. Now, I will shut up and get back to Dale and Jeff. We have been discussing the lovey dovey side of Dale and Jeff, so now let's do the flip side and get to the hatesy waitsy part of their life.

I could not count the number of times that I have been to the races and have heard the fan say that they hope that Dale and/or Jeff would get killed. That makes cold chills come over my body to know that some fans can have that much hatred in their hearts. I have heard fans call Jeff Gordon some of the worst names possible, while trying to spit on him. It really made me feel sorry for him. When Dale was killed I heard some fans that applauded when they found out he was gone. Some of the fans blamed the #40 driver and even made threatening phone calls to him. No one tried to wreck Dale. He was weaving back and forth in front of everyone tying to block for Dale Jr. and Michael. I loved Dale Earnhardt and he became my favorite driver when Richard retired in 1992. Even though he was my favorite driver, I will have to say that he took his own life by trying so hard to run interference for Dale Jr. and Michael. I am now a fan of Dale Jr. which was mostly carried over from his daddy. I hope the best of everything for Dale Jr and will be rooting for him at every race, but I also will never wish any bad luck on Jeff Gordon.

213

I hope you are enjoying my book and I don't mind if you think I am a dumb old hillbilly from Kentucky, that don't know when to shut up. Here is a big YeeHawee for you. Out of here.

The BUSCHWHACKERS

If you are a very dedicated Nascar fan you will have no problem knowing the definition of Buschwhackers. However, it you are virtually new to this great sport I will give you the definition to this word. A Buschwhacker is a Winston Cup driver that participates in the Busch Series race. So many fans have not liked the idea of Nascar letting the WC drivers drive in the Busch series. They seem to think it is unfair to the Busch driver, because the WC driver have more experience, better equipment, better crews and more money from a sponsor. Have you ever felt this way and wished the WC drivers were not allowed to drive in the Busch Series?

Well, listen up now, if you feel this way are you looking at the total picture and the bottom line which is money (MR. GREEN)? Please let me make this statement and elaborate on it by giving my opinion to how I feel about the Buschwhackers. Here is the statement that I want to make and it may shock you unless you see the total picture from the side of Nascar, track owners and sponsors. Here is the statement: IF THE WC DRIVERS DID NOT DRIVE IN THE BUSCH SERIES, THERE WOULD BE NO BUSCH SERIES. Hey now, you would probably say. How could that be true? I will answer that question for you and express my opinion; after all, this chapter is devoted to my opinions. I will try to explain and maybe even prove to you that there would be no Busch Series if the WC drivers could not be a part of it.

Before expressing my opinion you will need a little history lesson about the Busch and WC series of Nascar.

In the beginning of Nascar the WC series was called the Grand National Series. The Busch Series was called the Nascar Sportsman Series. Even from the beginning the Busch (NSS) Series was not profitable and was run as a companion race for the big WC race that was run on Sunday. The Busch Series was not a money maker, but it was simply used to bring more fans to the track and used as a promotion and advertising tool for WC. When the old names were changed to WC and NBS Nascar was beginning to evolve into a national sport instead of being know in the southern part of the USA only. The WC series was on top of the world and the seats were selling as quick as they could be built. However. this could not be said about the NBS. The seats were empty and the demand for tickets was at a all time low. It just seem that everyone was excited about the WC, but no one was interested in attending the NBS if they had to make a effort or go out of their way to attend it. The big majority of the fan that went to the NBS were fans that were already at the track to see the WC. It was very rare to see a fan drive any distance from home just to see the NBS race. It was getting to the point that Nascar could fill the seats for the WC race, but the NBS was still going broke. The track owners were loosing money on the NBS and was able to sell all of the tickets for the WC, therefore, not needing the NBS to promote the WC race. The track owners and Nascar were both in agreement that maybe they should abandon the NBS. Nascar met with several track owners and it was decided that the track owners put up appearance money to entice the WC drivers to be a part of the race. This was the plan for trying to save the NBS from going broke. At that time the track owners started paying the WC drivers about $10,000.00 just to appear and drive a car. Some of the drivers that were paid appearance money were. Mark Martin, Harry Gant, Dale Earnhardt, Jack Ingram and Darrell Waltrip. This proved to be the answer to the failing NBS. As soon as this program went into effect the seats started filling up and the Busch Series came back to life.

There you have it. Today the Nascar Busch Series if flourishing and the attendance has tripled all because of the appearance money that was paid to the drivers. When the tracks started making more more the purse started growing and the sponsors paid the teams more money. That is why the Busch Series is going strong today. I can remember that Randy Lajoie once said, that he didn't want to go to the WC series, because he would have to buy one of those expensive motorhomes and all of his expenses would increase so much that he could make more money in the Busch Series.

This is my opinion and I still think it is true today, when I say, If the WC drivers are not allowed to drive in the Busch Series, there would not be a Busch Series. What do you think? What is you opinion?

A CHAMPION OR A STROKER

As we all know, being a Nascar Champion is more about being consistent than winning races. I have never believed it was proper to crown a driver as the Nascar Champion just because he was consistent. In my opinion being consistent is almost like being a STROKER. Some of you younger fans may not know the definition of a STROKER because I haven't heard that word used in the racing world for more than 10 years.

A STROKER is an under financed driver that knows he has no chance of winning and just cautiously drives and tries to stay out of trouble in order to finish the race as close to the front as he can get. In the past there have been several very good drivers that were not able to prove their driving ability, due to lack of much need funds to built a top notch racing team. I have always favored and rooted for these drivers to finish well, because they had no other choice and would never be called the Nascar Champion. A big YeeHawee is in order for those STROKERS.

A STROKER and a Nascar Champion is not the same. However, if a driver only wins 1 race and wins the championship by being consistent, in my opinion he/she should in no way be the champion.

Yes, I do understand why Nascar has its system set up as such. They like to keep the points close until the last race of the season, which helps sell tickets. Nascar will also tell you it is because it helps distribute the money to the under financed teams. That is well and good as far as Nascar is concerned, but you must remember that it puts more money in their pocket.

In my opinion, I think the Nascar Champion should be the driver that wins the most races and not someone that had a good average finish.

I have a very good friend from Florida that I nicknamed Stan-Fan. We have shared our OPINIONS in regards to this matter and we certainly seem to think alike. Shown below are the feelings of my friend Stan-Fan.

Even as "milktoast" a spokesman for NASCAR's establishment as Benny Parsons is, he also has advocated a change in the points system to reward race wins, not consistency, as the measure for awarding the Winston Cup Championship. Matt had the wins last year - Tony Stewart had the consistency - however, Stewart is a much more electrifying personality than Matt Kenseth. NASCAR is not going to be able to market Matt around anything exciting, and that is the problem. Ryan Newman gets the most wins, and Junior and Jeff are the marquee stars of the sport. Veteran Bill Elliott remains competitive along with the talented Bobby Labonte. Up against that lineup, comes Kenseth, as bland and vanilla a personality as possible.

What NASCAR is selling is similar to football coaches (like a Dave Wannsteadt of the Miami Dolphins who play Not-To-Lose, instead of a John Gruden or Bill Parcells, who play To-Win Always). Fans are quickly going to lose interest in the sport with champions decided this way. MOF - probably most fans already have forgotten Kenseth. It isn't his fault, but nobody goes to a race, or tunes it in, to see their favorite driver run Top Five. They go to see their favorite driver win the race, and watch the predictable crashes no matter what any fan says to the contrary.

Parson's advocates consistency award points as 1/4 point, per lap led, per race, no matter how the driver finishes in the race, and a 50-point award for most wins, and winning, along with a bonus award for most poles, as qualifying and starting position are so important. Also a possibility is splitting the season into several segments, like The Winston is. Winner of each segment getting bonus points, but everyone starting over at zero each segment. You add in the segment's laps led, and victory bonus to final results at the end of the segment, for the four segments, possibly producing 4-different leaders, like playoffs, which prevents someone from building an insurmountable lead in September, and keeps the circuit, and championship race competitive to the end. No criticism of Matt is intended, he wins like everyone has won in the past. I am just thinking of the titles Bill Elliott and Rusty Wallace didn't win, when they dominated the circuit with 11-wins, and the points system prevented them from taking the title.

With every source in racing pounding on NASCAR's door to change the system, you would think they would hear it up there in Daytona Beach. They won't change a thing, however, until they discover that there is no market for a Matt Kenseth championship out there among the fans. He isn't the best driver on the circuit - by any stretch of the imagination - in 2003.

As NASCAR drops Winston and moves to Nextel, the time to change the system is upon them. With sponsors becoming scarce, the pressure to qualify and win is tremendous. The once exciting circuit has become vanilla bland - and that is something racing can never be. Time for a change. I have nothing against consistency - just reward it per race, no matter how the driver finishes, or award the Top Ten lap leaders with bonus points at the end of the season, based on individual race performance, no matter where they finish that particular race at, and put consistency second to race wins as the measure of a champion. Also, stop awarding points at the 25th finishing position. Every other sport does. Or, just forget about a champion, and let the sport run like golf, the only sport which runs competitive as long a season as NASCAR does and where there is no champion, just individual achievement, per match (same as per race), throughout the schedule. Granted there are big wins on the circuit Daytona, Darlington, Indianapolis, The Winston, Charlotte, just like there are major wins in golf, The Masters, U.S. Open, PGA and British Open. Done that way, in the end, there would be no question of the year's best driver. Nobody in golf is interested in who is the most consistent long driver, or putter on the circuit, or greens-hit-in-regulation, and that is a valid comparison of where NASCAR emphasis is, consistency, instead of winning the race (or in golf's case, the match). One way or the other, the bland season we just watched with Matt

Kenseth's championship will have one other effect, except making him rich. It is going to force NASCAR to change the rules - something they usually are not hesitant to do, in order to maintain their attendance and television audience, and sponsors.

DID YOU KNOW YeeHawee Style

THE BEST DAMN GARAGE IN TOWN

Written by Allen Madding speedwaymedia.com

At 957 North Beach Street in Daytona Beach, FL stands an old building with the windows painted over. Originally built to house a Laundromat, the building since 1947 has housed "The Best Damn Garage in Town" the garage of the legendary Smokey Yunick, one of the most colorful individuals to shape Motorsports history. Yunick died in May 2001 after battling cancer. His absence at the garage is noted by the eerie silence where for the last 50+ years the sounds of lathes, drill presses, and engine dynos signaled that the professor was at work. Yunick's trademark was his hat, white shirt and white pants. Never one to be politically correct, Yunick was an independent thinker, inventor, designer, engineer, and mechanic. Yunick's take on rulebooks was simple and to the point "If the rulebook didn't specifically outlaw this or that, then it was OK to do this or that." That stance didn't sit well with Bill France and NASCAR in the 1940's as the rulebook was very thin on specifics and most things fell under a blanket rule "the spirit of competition" which simply meant, Bill France could deem something illegal if he thought it would stink up the show. Smokey Yunick was notorious for stinking up a show and taking great pride in watching the sanctioning body squirm. A battle ensued between France and Yunick that continued for decades. Yunick maintained that if the rulebook did not specifically outlaw it, then he had to assume it was legal. France labeled Yunick's creativity "cheating". France began writing a rulebook to hem up Yunick. And Yunick gave France a lot of rules to write.

Yunick's Pontiac grabbed the pole at Daytona in 1959, 1961 and 1962. Those poles ruffled the feathers of the Chrysler and Ford factory backed teams who at the time practically owned the pole qualifying position. When Chrysler and Ford threatened to pull their support of NASCAR, France instructed his inspectors to nitpick Yunick's cars during the inspection process and a multi-decade feud between the Frances and Yunick ensued. Despite the quarreling between Yunick and the NASCAR establishment, as a car owner, Yunick captured 4 wins at Daytona Speedway between 1959 and 1962 and the NASCAR championship in 1952 and 1954. One of the most told stories of Yunick's creativity was controversy over the fuel mileage of one of Yunick's cars at Daytona. Rumor's swirled in the garage that the car had an over sized fuel tank. NASCAR removed the fuel tank and a heated argument ensued. Yunick became infuriated, crawled in the car, started it, and drove it back to his shop without a fuel tank. The car had an 11-foot fuel line that was 2 inches in diameter and held 6 gallons of gas. NASCAR quickly penned a rule restricting fuel lines to a maximum of 3/8 inches in diameter. Yunick's work was more far reaching than NASCAR however. Yunick was also involved for several years as a car owner at the Indy 500 where he also garnered a win in 1960.

The Best Damn Garage in Town became a testing and design facility for several manufacturers. General Motors sent numerous projects to Yunick including the 355 horsepower V6 that Yunick created for Buick in 1978. Over the years, the engineers at Chevrolet, Pontiac, Buick, Holley and others had learned the path to 957 North Beach Street Daytona Beach, FL. Millions of American racers and hot rodders sought out his advice thru the pages of Hot Rod Magazine and Circle Track Magazine. Yunick tried his best to answer every letter he received from the articles and even sent writers the phone number of his shop. When Yunick was diagnosed with cancer, he gave instruction to his family not to make a museum out of his shop but to sell it and the contents. The family has complied with his wishes, holding multiple garage sales with collectors from around the world buying tools, equipment, parts, and engines. What remains is the large shop complex sitting on 3 acres and "submerged land rights" that run underwater out to the channel in the Halifax River, something Yunick had wisely procured to allow for a large dock with very few permits required. The famous sign remains out front and the family says it will remain for Speedweeks so fans can stop by for a picture. The building and property were officially listed for sale on Wednesday, but the mark on Motorsports and Automotive development made by Smokey Yunick will endure for many years to come.

BROOKE and JEFF
http://www.geocities.com/winstoncup24/jeffbrooke.html

Let's start out with getting to know a little about Brooke. She grew up in Winston-Salem, NC and attended the University of North Carolina where she majored in Psychology and was a member of Chi Omega Sorority. Brooke was a model for Marilyn's Modeling Agency in Greensboro and worked on such accounts like Chachita Bananas. Right now she is a licensed Insurance Agent. Would you believe she was never a NASCAR fan? A friend of hers suggested that she interview to be a Miss Winston. For you newer NASCAR fans a Miss Winston's job is to appear at Winston Cup events, congratulate the winners in Victory Lane and they usually promote Winston Cup activities.

The first race she had ever seen was in 1992 for the Twin 125's qualifying - Jeff Gordon had won. As a unwritten rule, drivers are not allowed to have romantic relationships with a Miss Winston. This didn't matter to Jeff for he had called Brooke several times for a date. There were no results, she never called him back. On Valentine's Day 1992, before the Charlotte race Brooke Sealy and Jeff Gordon had finally met. She gave him some heart shaped candies for good luck and later on gave him the trophy. Using their young age as a total excuse, they would wink at one another and talk afterward. They had met up several other times such as a charity event and a autograph signing. By this time, they wanted to see more of each other. They started to date regularly in secret. They would meet up at odd times, duck in and out of side doors and go to places NASCAR crowds usually didn't. They had agreed if they were discovered - the relationship would be over until Brooke's year was over. We know how that turned out!!! When Jeff was 14, he had grown a pencil thin mustache that he enhanced with a eye brow pencil. To that day he had it. Several months into their courtship, Brooke asked if he would ever shave it off....to her surprise that same night, after a few minutes Jeff came back from the bathroom with his mustache shaved off. As they were dating, Brooke had to duck out back doors or kitchens when another driver came in. As well as on race weekends, she had to wait for other flights when a crew or driver showed up. One story to tell was as they were waiting to be seated, Kyle Petty came in - spotted Jeff and almost found out the identity of his date, but Jeff distracted him.

Another time was when another driver challenged Jeff because he was always alone and asked if he was gay. This buzzed around all season because no one understood why he always showed up to functions alone. Let alone why Brooke Sealy showed up alone. No one ever linked the 2 big stories together. At the end of the 93 season they were quite happy because now they wouldn't have to sneak around. They officially spoke out about their romance after the NASCAR Awards Banquet where Jeff won Rookie of the Year and Brooke's year was up. The following February in Daytona, before the Busch Clash - the "big question" was asked. No one really knows how Gordon did it. There are plenty of ideas floating around. But the result was the same, she accepted right away. Following Jeff would win the Busch Clash and won the 1st Winston Cup race at Charlotte.

They were married on November 26, 1994. Only family and friends attended. They had a 7 ft. wedding cake, and their picture on Carolina bride. Fans were able to mark the occasion with a donation to Jeff's favorite charity, The Leukemia Society of America. They bought a house alongside Lake Norman on the outside of Charlotte. It's said that Brooke has changed Jeff for the better. His driving improved, became more patient. When they aren't at the track, they are at their 4 bedroom mansion with their toys. Some are a 45 ft motorhome, a lear jet, 29 ft speedboat and a red Jaguar XX-8. When they are away from the track they spend a lot of time together playing basketball at home, doing water sports and playing some golf. They also go to the movies a lot. Since Jeff suffers from allergies - Brooke kids him about thats his way to get out of mowing the lawn. Both Jeff and Brooke are devoted Christians. They go to church regularly and Brooke can be seen praying for her husband before the race. She gave him a scripture that would go in the car with him; "3:5-6 Trust in the Lord with all thine heart; and lean not unto thine own understanding". Jeff is not only involved with Promise Keepers, he is active with charities such as Leukemia Society, Kids and the Hood, and Make a Wish Foundation. Coming to a halt, as everyone knows this year Brooke filed for divorce on Marital misconduct. She was looking to have almost everything. The story-book fairy tale has come to an end. We don't know what happened, but I think it would be very respectful to not ask questions. Most of their life was in the public eye - that should only ever go so far. Plenty say this has affected Jeff's driving which if you look it hasn't. He is a little distracted but not enough to stop him from searching out his 5th Championship. There are rumors going around that he's gay or went to another woman. But I will say this once. I believe all the rumors were started by anti-Gordon fans and if you are a "TRUE" Jeff Gordon fan you will stand behind him through all and never give up.

We may never know what exactly went on to cause their separation, and it was a shock to everyone to hear about it. We don't really know if they are still friends or work together or what is going on but they do.

DID YOU KNOW?

Here is a topic that I enjoy writing about. It helps me to remember and enjoy my happy days from yesteryear and it can refresh the memory of you long time fans and it will be a good learning tool for the newcomers to Nascar racing. Sit back, relax, be happy and have fun.

1. DID YOU KNOW? Tiny Lund was borne in Iowa, but moved to South Carolina where he and his family owned and managed a fish market and fish hatchery.

2. Many of you probably think that Bobby and Donnie Allison were borne in Alabama. They were both born in Florida. When they started racing on the short dirt tracks,

they found out about that the purses in Alabama being more than twice what they were in Florida. Off they went to try their luck at the Alabama tracks. They had very little money and had to live on peaches for 4 days.

3. One time back in the 50's Curtis Turner and Buck Baker were wrestling and horse playing on a front wooden porch that was not structurally sound. The floor broke through and both men tumbled to the ground. Curtis had a small splinter to stick in his eye and Buck had a broken finger.

4. Dale Earnhardt liked to pull pranks and tricks on Rusty Wallace. Rusty was trying to figure out a way to get even with Dale. The day came for Rusty and he had his chance to retaliate. Rusty went behind Dale's back when Dale wasn't looking and and took the steering wheel out of the car and put it in his car. When Dale got in his car it was almost race time and he had no steering wheel. Just a few minutes before it was time to start the engines, Rusty held the steering wheel out of his window and shook it at Dale.

5. Ned Jarrett use to me the manager of Hickory speedway and eventually became the owner. Later he sold the speedway.

6. Did you know that Buckshot Jone's daddy owns the controlling interest in Georgia-Pacific?

7. Can you remember Bobby Johns the driver from Florida? He use to drive the #7 car. If you can remember him well, you will remember those awful scars he had on his face. Those scars were caused by a cow that drug him through a barbed wire fence.

8. Do you mind if I take time out to tell you how much I enjoy writing these live articles. I GOT IT BAD. YeeHawee.

9. When PE was building a new garage, Kyle was a little boy at that time. The construction crew had just finished pouring a beautiful concrete floor. Kyle had a dog and somehow managed to get the dog to run across the concrete, then to cap it off, Kyle started chasing the dog through the wet concrete. BTW, have you heard people say that a car hit a cement wall. There is no such thing as a cement wall. Cement is one of the aggregates that is used in making concrete. Concrete is made up of cement, sand, gravel and water. cement, sand, gravel and water are the separate parts of concrete. Why do they say cement walls? They never say sand walls, or gravel walls or water walls?

10. One time at Talladega a intoxicated fan actually stole the pace car. About 45 minutes before the race was scheduled to start the pace car was parked near the entrance to pit road. The drunk fan jumped in the car and headed around the track to take a spin. The police and other security personnel tried to stop him when he came back by, but he just kept driving. Next, the police used about 10 cars as a road block and the drunk had to stop. He was jerked very furiously from the car and hauled off to jail. According to the paper the next day he was charged with several petty crimes, but to set an example they also charged him with a felony, which was Grand Theft Auto.

11. Sometime back in the 80's I went to the race in Atlanta with about 40 of my friends. We were on a

chartered touring bus. At that time the race at Atlanta was in August which was the hottest time of the year. It was so hot and dry that all of the grass was brown and almost dying. Our driver parked the bus and we all went inside the track. We had not been inside the track for more than 20 minutes when we saw a huge amount of smoke coming from the direction where our bus was parked. Some one accidentally caught the grass on fire and it spread so fast that it started burning the cars in the parking lot. Some of the car were exploding and it would catch others on fire. I never give statistics unless I am positive about the correctness of them, but about 30 cars and 5 motorhomes were destroyed.

12. Fred Lorenzen owned a real estate company and made millions of dollars during its prime. His biggest pay check came when his company and his associated started filling in the wetlands adjoining Lakeshore Drive in Chicago. When it was filled in building began to go up and his pocket book started to grow.

13. Wendell Scott had finally won his first race, at least that is what he thought. According to Nascar it showed that Wendell was not the winner. Wendell knew without a shadow of a doubt that he had won. However, there was nothing he could do about it at that time. Believe it or not, many years later Nascar awarded him as the winner of that race.

14. Ray Fox use to own the #3 Dodge that was driven by David Pearson, Buddy Baker, Charlie Glotzbach and others. During a certain year (?) there was a big demand of the top drivers of Nascar. All of the top drivers started leaving Ray Fox at about the same time in order to driver

for other car owners. During that year, about 15 different drivers drove the # 3 car.

15. I am sure that most of you can remember when Bobby Allison drove the Coke Cola car. At that time most of the driver wore plain looking driver uniforms and the crews also were wearing virtually plain pants and shirts. When Coke sponsored the car, Bobby was really dressed us fit to kill and his crew in their coke uniforms sure stood out from all the rest. I particularly loved their outfits, but it was the talk of the speedway. So many people were laughing and making mockery of them. Very soon every one else begin to stand out also.

RICHARD PETTY

1 Did you know Richard was called squirrel?
2 In the starting lineup of his first race he was listed at Dick Petty?
3 Richard has lost 50% of his hearing?
4 His eyes are very sensitive to light?
5 For his 1,000 WC start, his daughters gave command, To Start Engines.
6 He went out of his final race in a burning car.
7 He is afraid of flying.
8 Had a uncle named Julie.
9 He promised his mother that he would never have a alcohol sponsor.
10 His car was never in the Busch Clash or Bud Shootout.

DAVID PEARSON

1 Second winningest driver of all times.
2 His wife's name is Helen.
3 His son Larry drove a race car.

4 Was called the Silver Fox.
5 Won the 1976 Daytona 500 while crossing the finish line at 10 mph.
6 Was a driving instructor for Buckshot Jones.
7 He and Wood Brothers split in 1979.
8 Lived in Spartanburg, SC.
9 Drove only to the big tracks for several years.
10 Was considered the King of Darlington.

DARRELL WALTRIP

1 From Owensboro, KY.
2 His wife miscarried twice before having Jessica.
3 Stevie's dad was one of the first sponsors foe Darrell.
4 Jake Elder was his unpaid first crew chief at his first race at Talladega.
5 Cale Yarborough named him Jaws.
6 Was a superstar in the #88 Gatorade car.
7 He and Junior Johnson bought out his contract from Bill Gardner.
8 Some fans hated him so much that they would cheer when he had a violent wreck.
9 Won three championships for Junior Johnson.
10 His brother Michael lived with Richard Petty for 4 months.

CALE YARBOROUGH

1 Cale was a skydiver.
2 Semi-pro Football Player.
3 Crawled under the fence at Darlington to watch his first race.
4 Had a bunch of girls, but never did get a son.
5 Was only 5' 5" tall.

6 Was a big time business man and owned several businesses.

7 His car completely sailed over the wall at Darlington and out of the speedway.

8 Had a fight with both Bobby and Donnie Allison.

9 Won 2 back to back Daytona 500's.

10 Now lives in Sardis, SC

CHARLIE GLOTZBACH

1 Hometown is Georgetown, IN.

2 Was shot by one of his employees.

3 Was sponsored by Valleydale Meats.

4 Owned a trucking company.

5 Was known as Chargin Charlie.

6 Drove #3 Dodge for Ray Fox.

7 Drove #6 for Cotton Owens.

8 Drove #99 for Ray Nichols.

9 Won Bristol as a substitute driver.

10 Boycotted the first Talladega race and his car won the race and was driven by Richard Brickhouse.

TINY LUND

1 Was born in IA and moved to Cross, SC.

2 He was 6' 4" tall and weighed 300 pounds.

3 Won Daytona 500 in 1963 driving for injured Marvin Panch.

4 He owned a fish market.

5 Was killed on the backstretch at Talladega.

6 Use to carry Marty Robbins on his shoulders.

7 Broke Curtis Turner's arm.

8 Favorite car number was 16.

9 Best racing friend was Marty Robbins.

10 He never had a top notch car for most of his racing career.

SMOKEY YUNICK

1 Smokey was a mechanical genius.
2 The name of his garage in Daytona was called, "The Best Damn Garage in Town"
3 His most famous driver was Fireball Roberts.
4 He once built a car that would get over 100 miles per gallon.
5 It was said, that a oil company bought the patent to keep the car from being sold.
6 Smokey always spoke his piece regardless of who it hurt.
7 In my opinion he was the greatest race car mechanic in the world.
8 He even told the officials right to their face to Go to Hell.
9 Smokey was a very heavy cigar smoker.
10 He always wore the same of wide brim hat.

FRED LORENZEN

1 Was from Elmhurst, IL.
2 Drove # 28 blue and white Ford.
3 He was part of the Holman-Moody team.
4 He was known as a ladies man.
5 He was called the Golden Boy.
6 He retired in his 30's.
7 He tried to make a comeback while driving a Chevrolet for Junior Johnson at Charlotte.
8 He was considered one of Nascar's smartest drivers.
9 His hair was so blond that it looked golden.
10 He now owns a real estate company in IL.

CURTIS TURNER

1 His hometown was Roanoke, VA.

2 He loved the number 21.

3 He was a wealthy timber man before he started racing.

4 His best friend was Little Joe Weatherly.

5 He was a licensed pilot.

6 Crashed his plane and walked away twice.

7 Little Joe would start a fight and Curtis would help him.

8 His hardest competitive was Junior Johnson.

9 When Little Joe was killed at Riverside, Curtis said, I have just lost my brother and started crying.

10 Curtis was killed when he crashed his plane for the third time.

BUCK BAKER

1 Did you know his name was Elzie Wiley Baker.

2 Buddy was also name Elzie Wiley, II.

3 His biggest competitor was Tim Flock.

4 He loved the dirt tracks more than asphalt.

5 He was from Charlotte.

6 Started his own Buck Baker Driving School.

7 He won about 50 Nascar races.

8 After retiring from Nascar, he continues to drive GT car and others until he was in his 60's.

9 He said Buddy was a better driver than his record showed.

10 Buddy now helps him with his driving career.

LEE PETTY

1 Was born in Randleman, NC.

2 Married to Elizabeth.

3 Had a brother names Julie.

4 His son Maurice had polio.

5 He got the number 42 by looking at a license plate in the junk yard.

6 He started racing on the street for money.

7 Had a big fight with Tiny Lund.

8 He tried to be a race announcer, but failed.

9 He said Adam has the talent of Richard.

10 He was one of Nascar's hardest chargers.

DID YOU KNOW?
TODD BODINE IS A STAFF WRITER

From The Inside by Todd Bodine
www.catchfence.com/html/2003/tb103103.html

The NASCAR Winston Cup Series headed to Atlanta Motor Speedway last weekend, a track that is one of the fastest on the circuit. My career best finish in Winston Cup came at this Hampton, Georgia based track back in 1994 and as a team we headed into the track with all hopes of beating that on Sunday. In the first practice session the National Guard Ford was good. We were just a little on the tight side and we looked into camber, air pressure and shocks to help. We were fast and felt we had a good shot at qualifying. Sometimes at Atlanta qualifying mid pack is ideal. The humidity has a chance to build up the later you go in time trials. In our case it really didn't do it, but we didn't mind our qualifying draw of lucky 13. The speed charts clocked us going 191.814 miles per hour or 28.903 seconds in qualifying. The car was actually tight off both corners. I actually had to lift off a little bit coming out of turn four to keep from hitting the wall. It didn't hurt us that much because the car was fast enough. I think we could have had something for Elliott Sadler if we didn't have the pushing problem. That's racing, and that's the way it goes sometimes. The time should be good enough for a top 10, and it was for the second time in three weeks we were starting our No. 54 BELCAR Racing entry in the top ten. The car was good in the two remaining practice sessions of the weekend; we were looking forward to good results on Sunday. With inclement weather lurking, the race was started and we had moved up to fifth place in the opening laps. Despite the fast start, we were forced to drop back into 10th place on lap 20. I radioed in to Crew Chief Gary Cogswell that the car was handling tight through the middle and off of the corners. At the 51-mile mark, NASCAR threw the yellow flag after raindrops started dampening the track's surface. The front runners, including the No. 54 took the opportunity to pit under caution. In 17 seconds, the crew made an air pressure and wedge adjustment along with taking on four new Goodyears and fuel. Once the cars got realigned, the race was red-flagged due to rain showers. Unfortunately, the raced was called shortly after 6 p.m. and rescheduled for Monday morning at 11 a.m. Shortly after restarting the Bass Pro Shops MBNA 500 on Monday, the No. 15 car of Michael Waltrip broke loose entering the straightaway at Atlanta (Ga.) Motor Speedway. Waltrip's back end struck the No. 54 National Guard Ford sending it hard against the wall. The Guard car sustained serious damage and could not continue. I was transported to the infield care center where I was checked out and released. Car 54-finished 42nd. It's such a shame because we had such a good car. The best way I can describe what took place is it's just one of those racing deals. Michael did not come up into me. I think what happened is he simply got aerodynamically loose. It's typical because of the way our cars are designed. They are so aerodynamically dependent so when they get slightly upset, they really react. Michael's car was so sensitive on that first lap that he actually got into me two times. The first time, I was able to recollect it. Then the second time, my car just hooked around and went straight for the wall. There wasn't a thing I could do. When we took the green flag today, the car really stuck. I think what few adjustments we made on that first pit stop seemed to work. It's just so disheartening to see all the work we have done come to this. I said it last week and I'll say it again, we have a great group of guys assembled and we'll continue to work towards next season. We are not going to let the last two weeks get us down. We're moving on as the NASCAR Winston Cup Series heads to Phoenix International Raceway this weekend. In Phoenix we need to do everything we can to get the car to turn. It's the biggest thing I ask for when trying to get the car to handle the way I need it. Usually, my biggest complaint over the last couple of races has been tight in turns one and two. When it comes to turns three and four, we've been loose off. So, I have Gary (Cogswell) already thinking about ways we can combat those problems. If we can practice well, qualify up front and have a little luck on Sunday, we should be able to score a much-deserved top ten finish. The Winston Cup Series are ready to attack Phoenix International Raceway this weekend. The green flag for the Checker Auto Parts 500 drops shortly after 3:30 PM EST, with live coverage on NBC beginning at 3:00PM EST, with MRN radio also joining at 3:00 PM EST. I am hoping for a great race on Sunday and hope that you will be keeping an eye on the National Guard Ford along with your favorite driver(s). I'll talk to you next week and thanks for reading!

Todd Bodine.

JACK ROUSH CAT IN HAT

Matt Kenseth has won the 2003 Nascar Winston Cup Championship. This is the first time that Jack Roush has won the championship as a car owner. Hey, let's wait just a minute. Sure, it is Jack's team. sure Jack deserves the championship, but technically Matt Kenseth's car is owned by Mark Martin and I am sure that Mark will be please to see THE CAT IN THE HAT receive the trophy. Omer

Hats Off To The Cat

by Paul Miron-Staff Writer

At race's conclusion on Sunday, Jack Roush was speechless- for a moment. Four-time runner-up in the title chase, Roush Racing finally secured a Cup and Jack had no words to describe the moment. Then, The Cat in the Hat began meowing again- templates, addressing the approval of the new Ford cylinder head. That crusty survivor never shut up, takin' it to the house. He took it home but he wouldn't close his trap. Leopards are cats, right? Never change their spots. What about jaguars? Matt was a jaguar this season. He sneaked up on 'em, playing cool and cagey, scoring one mere hit but a slew of near-misses and he won't go home hungry. NASCAR pays points for near-misses and this cat used up his Goodyears and uncanny racing luck to clinch the Cup. There are those who'd call Kenseth's championship a fluke but NASCAR sets the rules, God intervenes- and all is well. The NASCAR family nearly lost Jack last year but God had another calling for him- Roush's work on Earth wasn't done. A mere mortal would have certainly perished under other circumstances but divine intervention brought Jack back- to the chagrin of his opponents, to NASCAR, all the way to the banquet this year. It makes one wonder- does NASCAR have a red phone linked upstairs? Does God love cats? Is Jack really a cat? The Cup is not a gift, it's a reward for hard work and dedication in a sport of precision, luck, faith and love. Stop whining, Jack, and pray to God. Sip from the Cup, dwell on your success, take off your hat and thank the Lord that you were given a ninth life. As Dear Abby used to say- kwitcherbitchin. Hats off to the Cat in the Hat and his cagey sidekick. Opponents, keep your notes handy. Pet your cat and go to church. Jack's quietly working with a jag that doesn't change its spots. Jack, leave your hat on- it covers a never-ending think-tank, starved and finally rewarded, but your work is not yet done. The Hat, the complainer, the whiny cat in the corner...there's another cup of milk for you next year. Suddenly, every NASCAR team has a cat in its garage. The Cat's working with a jaguar whose spots don't change. Congratulations to Roush Racing - to Matt Kenseth and to the Cat in the Hat. Your precision and luck, accompanied by proper planning and execution have combined for a decisive championship run. Hats off to the Cat - thank God.

You can reach Paul Miron at: pmiron@catchfence.com

HOW TO WRITE RACING ARTICLES.

DID YOU KNOW there is someone willing to help you learn to be a good writer of racing stories. Do you think you are a good writer, or maybe you would like to become one. If you are interested in learning to be a good writer, I suggest you read the article below. Omer

HOW TO WRITE RACING ARTICLES
www.wrecksnrants.com/newsletters/issue1.html
by Don Terrill http://www.racingsecrets.com

For a couple years now I've tried to get people to write for my websites. The only thing I've accomplished is wasted breath. Maybe it's just me, but trying to get people to do anything seems to be impossible these days~even if it's for their own good, they still won't do it. Am I ranting? Sorry, it's just I know how good most people's writing skills are~a lot better than mine~and they still won't write. Well, if you'd like to prove me wrong about people, here's your chance.

Below is some guidance on writing your first racing article: (not that you need any) Force yourself to write ~ Writing something, anything, is better than writing nothing at all. Just sit down and write, don't worry about spelling or punctuation. Your goal is to get the mush in your head, out.

Write comfortably ~ For me it's just a pen and paper. Even though I've got many computers, including a laptop, I still find it easier to write on paper. Find what works best for you. Make it informative ~ No one wants to read about your trip to the Daytona 500. We want knowledge, advice, tips, anything that will make our lives better. For some of us, racing is our life. Here's the kind of content you should have in your article: How to information ~ Teach the reader how to do something, or teach them what not to do.

Resources ~ Tell readers where they can buy the items mentioned in your article; list websites, part numbers, etc. Make it easy to read ~ Most people's attention spans are too short to read things completely, they want to be able to scan the material for the highlights. Use the following three tips to make it easier on them.

Bullets ~ They help to draw attention to key points. Small paragraphs ~ It's a lot easier to read when text is broken up into small sections. Most people won't even read text that's one long paragraph.

Narrow text wrap ~ This refers to how many characters on a line before it wraps to the next line. When you use long lines it's easy for readers to lose their place.

Don't be afraid to give the goods ~ One thing I've learned over the years is how few people will actually take your advice and put it to good use. I'd say it's less than 1%. So, show the world how smart you are (Don't worry, nobody will do anything with the info anyway).

Forget perfection ~ If you wait for perfection, you'll never get anything done. This used to be my problem, not any more, now I understand the importance of finishing. Anyway, I think the writer will always be more critical of his own work. Readers are more concerned about content, not style. Use an outline ~ Yes I know, you hated them in school. Still, outlines are the best way to write. I start with the title and just break it down form there; subheadings next; and then the paragraphs themselves. This way I'm just concentrating on one part at a time, not the entire project.

Did you find some mistakes in this article? Want to send me an email telling me how poor my writing skills are? That's fine, at least I wrote something.

Article by DON TERRILL of RacingSecrets.com. Don is a three time poll winning Winston cup engine builder. Visit http://RacingSecrets.com for more "how-to" on Racing. Don't have time to visit the site? Subscribe to their Free, monthly newsletter: mail to: RacingHelp@GetResponse.com This article courtesy of http://www.wrecksnrants.com

PICTURES YeeHawee Style

YEEHAWEE. Omer Champion's world famous HILLBILLY GRILL. When I go to the races I usually camp. I would take a charcoal grill with me to use for cooking. I would stand it up inside the van and try to prop it up with other camping gear to keep it from falling over. However, that didn't work because the grill keep falling over and the ashes and grease started to ruin my van. I decided to not take the whole charcoal grill with me but only take the metal grill alone. I took the grill rack and put it in a black garbage bag and tied it up in order to keep everything clean. When I got to the campground and set the grill up it was so simple and everything worked super. I would pour the charcoal out on the bare ground, stand up 4 aluminum cans and sit the grill on top of the cans. I could sit in the grass and be the best chef at the campground. When it was time to go home and the grill was cool, I simply slid the grill back into the garbage bag and had a very CLEAN trip back to Kentucky. Some may say that necessity is the mother of invention, but here in Kentucky we call it HILLBILLY HAPPINESS.

Racing University
has conferred upon
Omer Champion
the degree of
Bachelor of Speed
with all the rights, privileges and honors pertaining thereto.
In testimony whereof, the undersigned have hereunto
affixed their signatures and the seal of Racing University this
tenth day of February, nineteen hundred and seventy nine.

Dean   President

CERTIFICATE. For the last 46 years I have been answering questions for my Nascar friends. They have given me the nickname NASCAR PROFESSOR. Due to this nickname my friends presented me with this Racing University Certificate. Certificate By Larry Lange DE3FAN

Lowe's Motor Speedway 10/11/2003

Photo by Larry Lange ©2003

RICHARD CHILDRESS built this special car as a tribute to Dale Earnhardt. The car was unvailed at Charlotte in 2003 and driven around the track by Richard Childress. Photo by Larry Lange DE3FAN

The Earnhardt Legacy

© 2002

EARNHARDT FAMILY. This is a collage of the
Earnhardt Family. Does this make you wonder why Kerry
Earnhardt is not in this picture? Photo by Larry Lange
DEI3FAN

1967 Bristol Win.

Richard Petty. This picture of Richard Petty was taken at Bristol in 1967. This was Richard Petty's greatest year when he won 27 races which included10 races in a row. Jeff Dye gave me this picture. My friends are so special to me. Thank you Jeff. Omer

What a beautiful lady we see here in this picture. Richard Petty became so famous that he was called THE KING. Richard and all of his fans including me, owe a great debt of gratitude to Elizabeth Petty. Without THE QUEEN MOTHER there would have never been a Richard Petty. YeeHawee to the First Lady of racing, THE QUEEN MOTHER. Photo by Jeff Dye

Traveling from Iowa to Tennessee. This is my good friend Bob Perkins. Bob flew from Iowa to Knoxville where he rented a motorhome to drive to Bristol for a four day stay with me at Camp YeeHawee. When you consider the price of the Airplane, Motorhome, Tickets, Camping and additional expenses it cost Bob more than $3,000.00. This will answer our question of HOW BAD DO YOU HAVE IT? Photo by Bob Perkins.

YEEHAWEE. JEFF GORDON, A STAR IS BORN. This is the young Jeff Gordon kneeling beside his #1 Baby Ruth BGN Ford. This Ford was owned by Bill Davis. Later Jeff Gordon joined the team owned by Rick Hendrick and became famous driving a Chevrolet. This picture was taken during his rookie year in Nascar. Photo by StanFan

Friends at Camp YeeHawee. From left to right: Troy, Scott,my son Champ, Sue, Omer, George and Charles. Photo by Jen.

"GOD SENT ME AN ANGEL" Jo and I have been married over 40 years and are still like two little LOVE BIRDS, except our feathers are a little wrinkled. GOD sure has blessed me during my lifetime, but the best blessing I have ever received was when HE sent me my ANGEL. I love you Jo!

Does anyone know who that young man is with THE GIRL NAMED SUE? I hope that someday he will be as famous as Sue. Sue imigrated to the United States when she was 15 years old. Let me tell you folks, her blood is red, white and blue. It is no wonder that we have open borders. I wish we had a million more like her. A big YeeHawee is in order for A GIRL NAMED SUE. Photo by Sue Honoski.

RICHARD PETTY and my very good friend Scott. Scott has an awesome collection of Nascar pictures. Scott is also from Kentucky, but I consider him a northern HILLBILLY. Photo by Scott Flack.

YEEHAWEE to the happy days. This is a picture of Brook and Jeff. At that time Brook was Miss Winston and Jeff was a young kid that was kicking butts in Winston Cup racing. When they met in victory lane they started dating and were married soon thereafter. However, the marriage ended in a bitter divorce. Photo by Stan Fan.

YeeHawee Gang. What a great day this was at Camp YeeHawee. Twenty three of my YeeHawee Friends met me at Bristol in 2002. We had such a great time especially when we had a Show and Tell. That was the day that Jeff showed me the 1967 picture of Richard Petty. Later on he gave me the picture. From left to right is Mikc, Tina, Jeff, Omer, Scott and Charles. Photo by Champ

YeeHawing Down in Bristol. This is what we all call YeeHawing Down in Bristol. It is no wonder that I am the happiest man in the world because of friends like these. From left to right: my son Lt. Omer Champion, ll, Charles, Jim, Rita, Omer and Scott. This was the day that my friend Jim, gave a tape of a song he sang and played for me. The title was YeeHawing Down in Bristol. Thanks Jim, you are my buddy.

YEEHAWEE for Ronald McDonald. It is hard to explain how much fun we have at Camp YeeHawee. Two years ago there were 23 of us together and we had a show and tell. The picture you see here was Dave R. Porter sporting a Ronald McDonald outfit. In Dave's younger years he entertained the kids as a Ronald McDonald clown. This is what he brought to show and tell. It is no wonder that we have Dr. Ray camping with us, because someone has to keep this crazy bunch from destroying themselves.

Petty / Earnhardt

RICHARD PETTY and Dale Earnhardt are without a doubt, two of the greatest Nascar drivers of all times. They have both won 7 Winston Cup Championships. Richard has won 7 Daytona 500's. Dale had many runs of bad luck and it took him 20 years to finally conquer the Daytona 500 in 1998. Photo by Mickey Weinstein, www.instantreplaysportscard.com